W9-AVL-723

Use Your Brain
to Be Your Best Self &
Create Your Ideal Relationship

EMPOWERED
LOVE

Steven Stosny, Ph.D.

ixia
PRESS

Mineola, New York

Bibliographical Note

Empowered Love: Use Your Brain to Be Your Best Self and Create Your Ideal Relationship is a new work, first published by Ixia Press in 2018.

International Standard Book Number

ISBN-13: 978-0-486-81940-2
ISBN-10: 0-486-81940-X

IXIA PRESS
An imprint of Dover Publications, Inc.

Manufactured in the United States by LSC Communications
81940X01   2017
www.doverpublications.com/ixiapress

For Fang Peng, my light

TABLE OF CONTENTS

Love Relationships: A World of Their Own

In more than a quarter-century of clinical practice, I've been fascinated, troubled, and occasionally tormented by three questions:

Why do so many smart and creative people make the same mistakes over and over?

At what point does the unavoidable emotional pain of life become entirely avoidable suffering?

How do we avoid suffering, while remaining vibrant and passionate about life?

I explored these questions in a previous book, *Soar Above: How to Use the Most Profound Part of Your Brain Under Any Kind of Stress.* When under persistent stress, all animals, including humans, retreat to previously acquired habits. In the stresses of modern living most of us invoke conditioned emotional responses formed as far back as toddlerhood. These conditioned responses originate in the *Toddler brain* (fully developed on a structural level at age three), pretty much guaranteeing that we'll make the same emotional mistakes again and again, and run the risk of turning pain into suffering. *Soar Above* shows how to develop habits of coping in ways that activate the more profound upper prefrontal cortex: the *Adult brain*, which is fully developed around age 28. Used consistently, these new habits lead to greater interest, vibrancy, and success in most work and social contexts.

The Special Challenges of Love Relationships

I realized fairly early in writing *Soar Above* that I had to write a separate book to accommodate the special challenges of committed love relationships. These occur on an altogether different playing field from those of work and social life. As we'll see, many of the problems of love relationships stem from partners who behave at home in ways that might serve them well in work and social gatherings but fail miserably in love relationships. No important human endeavor makes it harder to stay consistently in the profoundest part of the brain than interactions with loved ones. The simple explanation of why this is so is that living with someone invokes a wide array of routine behaviors, running on autopilot, without forethought or conscious intention. Routine ways of behaving are likely to stimulate old emotional habits when stressors are added to the mix, such as quarreling children, urgent text messages from work, or overdue bills. The Toddler brain by habit looks for someone to blame, denies responsibility, or avoids the issue altogether.

The more subtle reason that we're apt to invoke Toddler-brain habits in committed relationships lies at the very heart of love. The same quality that makes love wonderful—giving fully of the deepest parts of ourselves—also makes it a little scary. Most lovers have not felt so emotionally dependent and powerless over their deepest vulnerable feelings since they learned to walk. Similarities in vulnerability can fool the brain under stress and increase the likelihood of invoking Toddler-brain ways of coping in love relationships. Most of the hundreds of couples I've treated were fine at work and with friends, smart, resourceful, and creative. But at home they were like playground kids pointing out each other's faults: "It takes one to know one!" Most were compassionate and kind to other people, but to each other they were opposing attorneys in a bitter lawsuit.

As we shall see, one of the reasons that love relationships are so hard is because falling in love is so easy. Powerful hormones and neurotransmitters heighten our senses, activate primal drives, and lower our defenses; to a large extent they *make* us fall in love. Despite the enormous complications of modern relationships, the human brain really *wants* to love.

Alas, the biology that brings us together doesn't keep us together. In fact, biology makes it more difficult to live together in happiness for more than a few years. That's probably because the biological underpinnings of emotional bonds evolved at a time when humans were tribal, not pair-bonded. Maintaining communal connection was more important to survival than sustaining intimate connection. The focus of two individuals on each other was to reproduce, not to build a life together, as we now desire.

Of course biology is only part of the story. The social and cultural factors that at one time helped sustain long-term relationships have now become a hindrance to them. For instance, marrying for love is relatively recent in human history. Up until a couple hundred years ago, marriage was entirely a political, social, or familial arrangement. A higher authority would commit you to a union with a person you hardly knew. Sometimes

you wouldn't even see your betrothed until the wedding cere-
mony. "Lifting the veil" was often the first time the betrothed
were face to face. Many people retain that tradition, along with
not allowing the groom to see the bride on their wedding day,
even when they've been living together for several years.

In the past, two people with very low levels of interest, trust,
compassion, and love for each other agreed to form a union
and build a life together. From such a low emotional starting point, there's nowhere to go but up. In modern times, we
start from very high levels of interest, trust, compassion, and
love, unsustainable levels given the focus and energy they consume. For us, there's nowhere to go but down.

The loss of infatuation is typically the first crisis of love
relationships, occurring by the second year of living together. If
couples do not cope with this crisis in the more profound areas
of their brains—the *Adult* brain—the guilt, shame, and anxiety
that emerge automatically as emotional bonds fade will turn
into resentment, anger, and, eventually, contempt.

An unforeseen but devastating pressure on long-term
love relationships came from the precipitous decline of the
extended family in the United States. As recently as a couple of
generations ago, the nuclear family—two parents and children
living alone together—was a rarity. Typically, grandma was
upstairs, Aunt Sally was in the basement, and Uncle Fred
was in the spare room. If they weren't under the same roof,
they were next door or across the street. Extended families
afforded couples much-needed support with children and
finances. Nearly as important, members of the extended family
were often emotional confidants for beleaguered spouses.
Unlike their predecessors, couples trying to maintain intimate
relationships now are quite òn their own.

Other cultural changes in recent decades have increased the pressure on modern intimate relationships, but those do not include the breakdown of traditional gender roles, as is sometimes mentioned in the press. Egalitarian behaviors have proved liberating and beneficial in love relationships. The more egalitarian— shared power, choices, and control of resources—the more likely relationships are to be happy. Rather, the negative effects of cultural change come in no small part from the radical transformation of expectations that couples bring to committed unions, particularly over what intimate partners should do for each other.

The family historian Stephanie Coontz has written two excellent books on the social and psychological changes in marriage, *Marriage, A History* and *The Way We Never Were*. She points out, for example, that women of a couple of generations ago would be appalled at the suggestion that they consider their male partners as emotional confidants. Women of years past generally regarded their husbands as the last people they would speak to about anything emotional. Only after testing the waters with girlfriends, sisters, aunts, and mothers might they mention emotional issues to their male partners. They simply did not believe husbands could understand the complexity of their feelings.

Of course, wives of those times didn't understand their husbands any better than their husbands understood them. The cultural shifts since those times have produced major changes in roles and expectations, with only slight improvement in understanding.

Partners *can* understand each other's emotional complexity and form a more perfect union, but only when they interact from the Adult brain. In the Toddler brain, neither has a chance of understanding the other.

The painful disconnection that modern intimate partners constantly confront rises from attempts to get their partners to do something—"meet my needs"—when both are in their Toddler brain. In the Toddler brain, they're incapable of seeing, much less helping, each other.

Habit vs. Love

In familiar environments, most of what we do is on auto-pilot, activating strings of habits that consume far less energy than consciously decided behavior. Each time we repeat the autopilot behavior, we strengthen the neural connections that activate it. More pointedly, habits rule under stress, when the mental resources required for consciously decided behaviors are taxed. The default to past habits when things get tough presents a major problem in sustaining feelings of love, interest, compassion, and trust.

Most of our emotional responses have been conditioned and shaped into habits *before* the profound part of the brain—the upper prefrontal cortex—is fully developed. (It's not completely articulated until the third decade of life.) Without the hormones and neurotransmitters of love overriding those habits (as they do when falling in love), we make the same self-centered mistakes again and again. As we shall see, we're apt to blame, criticize, evade, or stonewall when stuck in the Toddler brain, even though we know on some level that blaming, avoiding, criticizing, and stonewalling make situations worse and erode the emotional bond that holds couples together.

Power Love

In Part II of this book, we'll see how *Power love* invokes the profoundest part of the brain to transcend the limits of emotional habits and help us become the most empowered and humane partners we can be. *Power love* is a relationship based on desire rather than emotional need, on support rather than demands, on enduring values rather than temporary feelings.

Not that things won't go wrong in *Power love*. When they do, we'll be aware that we're not simply irritated or angry or anxious or sad, we're irritated, angry, anxious, or sad at someone we love and value. We'll always be aware that the love and value are more important than transitory negative feelings. We'll appreciate that loved ones are more cooperative when treated with compassion, kindness, and respect than when confronted with criticism and demands.

At the outset, consider which of the following is more likely to elicit cooperation from your partner and improve your relationship:

Toddler brain: "Do what I want or I won't love you."

Adult brain: "Let's do what makes us both feel valued and respected."

Power love nurtures individual growth and relationship accord, much like musicians in a duet. Both must practice their own instruments to perform well as a unit. Only then can they fit their individual resonances together to accomplish something greater than either can do separately. Together, they are empowered to make *harmony—empowered to act their most profound selves.*

PART I
Toddlers in Love

CHAPTER ONE

Love in the Wrong Part of the Brain

We fall in love in the *Toddler brain*, the wonderful, emotional, impulsive, and volatile *limbic system*, which reaches full structural maturity by age 3. We stay in love in the profoundest and most stable part of the *Adult brain*—the *prefrontal cortex*, which reaches full maturity around age 28. Toddler-brain love is filled with wonder and joy at first, but, as we shall see, inevitably causes irreconcilable conflict and pain due to its cognitive limitation, especially the inability to see other perspectives. Adult love rises from our deepest, most humane values of compassion, kindness, nurturance, and desire for mutual growth.

Most people would agree that, despite the moodiness and occasional temper tantrum, toddlers are joyous, loving, fascinating, and fun. And that sounds a lot like a description of falling in love, doesn't it? Toddler love can be lots of fun for adults when they emphasize curiosity, wonder, and affection. But when we retreat to the Toddler brain under stress, as we're wont to do, we become impulsive, reactive, self-obsessed, and demanding.

You may have noticed that you and your partner are more likely to shift into the Toddler brain in reaction to each other than in any other kind of relationship. You can be a sophisticated adult at work, in friendships, and at parties. So why is it so darn hard to maintain Adult-brain behaviors at home?

For all the wonderful things it adds to our lives, love exposes our deepest vulnerabilities, in ways that most of us haven't experienced since toddlerhood. In early relationship conflict, when habits of interacting are formed, most lovers have not felt so emotionally dependent and powerless over their deepest, most vulnerable feelings since they learned to walk.

Toddlers are powerless over their own emotional states, yet they wield a great deal of power to make people around them feel good or bad. Adults who love like toddlers make each other feel bad simply by having interests, tastes, and vulnerabilities that fail to mirror the fragile sense of self embedded in the Toddler brain. Most complaints in toddler love take the form of:

"Why can't you be more like me? Why can't you know what I need and just do it?"

Confusing intimacy with having their partners think and feel the same way they do, they perceive rejection and betrayal when loved ones think and behave like the unique individuals they are.

Love Comes Easy to the Toddler Brain

You may have heard the saying, "Love is easy; relationships are hard." The truth is, relationships are hard *because* love is so easy in the Toddler brain. In the beginning, euphoria and boundless energy flow from hormones like oxytocin and vasopressin, which are instrumental in social behavior, sexual motivation, and pair bonding. They make you feel like you're walking on clouds and barely have to eat or sleep. And then there's the hyperfocus of newly acquired love; you can think of little else besides the beloved. You can tell the "in love" couples in a restaurant; they're so into each other, they barely pick at their salads, oblivious to the sights and sounds around them.

Lacking the ability to make social inferences based on evidence, the Toddler brain relies on *projection* to discern other people; that is, Toddler brains attribute their own emotional states and unconscious impulses to others. Love makes the Toddler brain attribute our best feelings and ideals to our new objects of fascination. We focus on what we like, while pretty much ignoring what we don't like.

As the bonding hormones that brought us together wane (they can only last a few months), the euphoric feelings of falling in love fade. We stop the idealistic attributions and begin to see things in our lovers we don't like. It's not so much that we don't like who our lovers really are, it's just that previously they seemed to be everything we really liked.

If we just stopped the idealistic attributions, it wouldn't be so bad. But the self-obsessed Toddler brain cannot stop projecting. When it feels bad, it projects negative qualities onto the now disappointing loved one. The inevitable disillusionment is what couples begin to fight about, as early as the second year of living together. They struggle, in the wrong part of their brains, to balance what I call the *Grand Human Contradiction*.

The Grand Human Contradiction

Human beings are unique among animals in the need to balance two opposing drives. The drive to be *autonomous*—able to decide our own thoughts, imagination, creativity, feelings, and behavior—must compete with an equally strong drive to *connect* to significant others. We want to be free and independent, without feeling controlled. At the same time, we want to rely on significant others—and have them rely on us—for support and cooperation.

Other social animals—those who live in groups and packs and form rudimentary emotional bonds—have relatively little or no discernible sense of individuality to assert and defend. Solitary animals are free and independent but do not form bonds with others that last beyond mother-infancy. Only humans struggle with powerful drives that pull us in opposite directions, where too much emotional investment in one area impairs emotional investment in the other.

Competition between the drives for autonomy and connection is so important that it emerges in full force in toddlerhood, which is why "the twos" can be so "terrible." Toddlerhood is the first stage of development in which children seem to realize how separate they are from their caretakers, when they become aware of emotional states that differ from those of their parents. They had previously felt a kind of merging with caregivers, which provided a sense of security and comfort. The new realization of differences stirs excitement and curiosity but also endangers the comfort and security of the merged state. Now they must struggle with an inchoate sense of self prone to negative identity; that is, they don't know who they are, but when aroused, they know who they're not—they're not whatever you want. Thus we have the favorite two words of the toddler: "Mine!" and "No!"

The increasing conflict with parents wrought by the drive for autonomy endangers the other powerful human drive: to connect, to value and be valued, to be comforted and to comfort. Hostility toward their parents, however short in duration, stirs uncomfortable feelings of guilt, shame, and anxiety, which fuel intense emotional distress—the classic temper tantrum. Internal conflict is overwhelming for toddlers, because they have so little development in the regulatory part of their brains—the prefrontal cortex.

The Two Brains

The primary survival function of the Toddler brain is to generate an alarm. Toddlers can't take care of themselves, solve problems, or keep themselves safe. Their negative emotions are alarms to summon adults who will do those things for them.

All alarm systems, negative feelings included, are calibrated to give false positives. You don't want a smoke alarm that doesn't go off until the house is in flames; you want it to go off when there's just a little smoke, even if that means it occasionally gets triggered when someone is cooking or having a cigarette. The Toddler brain functions as if the smoke alarm *is* the fire, instead of a signal that a fire might possibly exist. That's like hearing a smoke alarm and screaming, "We're all going to die!" We actually come close to that level of error by assuming that Toddler-brain emotional alarms represent certain reality.

The Adult brain reacts to smoke alarms by checking out the signal to see if there really is a fire or just something cooking. If there is a fire, the focus is on putting it out, rather than reacting in panic, trying to ignore it, or blaming it on someone. In the Adult brain we pay attention to feelings as important signals but don't validate them as reality. Negative feelings are regulated with reality checks (is there really a fire?) *and* plans for improvement (put out the fire).

In addition to reality testing, the primary features of the Adult brain are appraisal, calculation, judgment, self-regulation (of emotions and impulses), and what psychologists call *theory of mind*, which is the ability to reflect on mental states of self and others. With these tools it interprets and explains experience: This is why I feel this way.

Most important in regard to love relationships, the Adult brain creates value. *Creating value* is holding persons (objects and ideas) as important and worthy of appreciation, time, energy, effort, and sacrifice. In the process of creating value, the Adult brain constructs the meaning of our lives.

The Toddler brain is impulsive, simplistic, self-obsessed, and given to power struggles: "Mine!" and "No!" Most relevant when it comes to maintaining love relationships, the Toddler brain is subject to splitting—all-or-nothing, black-and-white thinking. You're all good when I feel good, and bad when I don't; you're interesting when I feel vibrant, and dull when I feel bored. In the Adult brain, we can regulate negative feelings and impulses, integrate enjoyment and disappointment, see other perspectives, and analyze our own experience. There we can plan, weigh evidence, make sound judgments, and build a life of value and meaning.

Most parents recognize that toddlers have a very low tolerance for discomfort and frustration. We monitor their physiological states to be sure that they are rested, hydrated, and fed, to prevent sulking or temper tantrums when the least thing goes wrong. Most of their discomfort is physiological, but a significant portion comes from their struggles with the Grand Human Contradiction; it's hard for them to feel autonomous and connected at the same time. Only the Adult brain can accomplish that.

The downside of late maturity in the Adult brain (in the *third* decade of life) is that it comes online long after the

Toddler brain has already formed habits of coping with the alarms it raises, mostly through blame, denial, and avoidance. Under stress, these fortified neural patterns, reinforced countless times over the years, hijack higher cognitive processes. Instead of modifying Toddler-brain alarms with assessments of reality, the hijacked prefrontal cortex validates its alarms and justifies its impulsivity and overreactions.

To the extent that Toddler-brain habits are reinforced in adulthood, distorting the interpretations and explanations of the Adult brain, we confuse the alarm with reality. This confusion makes Toddler-brain alarms self-validating:

"If I'm angry, you must be doing something wrong."

"If I'm anxious, you must be threatening, rejecting, or manipulative."

"If I'm uncomfortable, you must be failing me."

If the couple remains in the Toddler brain, the blamed partner will inevitably blame back, creating resentment, hostility, and greater distance between them.

It's All About Feelings

Toddler love is all about feelings, with no sense of deeper values to guide or anchor them. In the Toddler brain we vacillate between autonomy and connection; sometimes we feel like losing the self in the relationship and sometimes we feel like sacrificing the relationship for self-indulgence. The popular culture has come up with a label that covers both vacillations: "Getting your needs met." Of course, the "needs" we want to get met are the competing drives of the Grand Human Contradiction, which, when out of balance, necessarily gives us a hot-and-cold, on-and-off relationship style. (Don't worry, Part II of this book will show how to keep them in balance.)

Feelings processed primarily in the Toddler brain are highly volatile, leaping from the very positive to the very negative without a moment's notice. This is what psychologists call "splitting" (the wellspring of "all-or-nothing" thinking). You're either all good or all bad; I love you or hate you; I think the best about you or the worst. You're on a pedestal when I feel good and you're a demon when I feel bad. I appear needy or aloof. I either cling or pout. If my feelings are hostile, I'm prone to passive aggression, abuse, and even violence.

Why Toddler Love *Must* Turn Negative

Did you ever wonder why people are more likely to notice things that stir negative emotion than those that might invoke a positive response? I don't just mean the "negative people" who constantly look for the possibility of a dark cloud somewhere amid silver linings. On autopilot, we all give disproportional weight to the negative. Consider how much time and energy you devote to recalling and thinking about negative experiences compared to the positive.

Emotions have what psychologists call "negative bias." Negative emotions get priority processing in the brain because they're more important for immediate survival. They give us the instant adrenaline jolt we need to avoid snakes in the grass and fend off sabertooth tigers, at the cost of noticing the beauty of our surroundings.

Ironically, positive emotions are more important to long-term well-being. You'll live longer and be healthier and happier if you experience considerably more positive emotions than negative ones. Life is better for those who are able to appreciate the beauty of the rolling meadow and the sun dappling the edges of surrounding trees, as long as they are able to notice the snake in the grass, too. We have to survive the moment to appreciate the world around us.

Negative bias is why loss causes pain disproportionately to the joy of equivalent gain. Having a nice meal is enjoyable but, in most cases, is incomparable to the distress of missing a meal altogether. Finding $10,000 will be pleasant for a day or so; losing $10,000 can ruin many, many days. More poignantly, having a child is a joyous occasion; losing a child takes a lifetime of recovery.

In my Toddler brain, the negative bias of emotions makes it unlikely that I'll notice all the things my partner does that benefit me (appreciation is the province of the Adult brain), but I'll surely resent when she doesn't do what I want. In family relationships, research shows that it typically requires at least five positive gestures to counterbalance one little negative remark. If research just measured Toddler-brain exchanges, the ratio of positive to negative no doubt would be higher just to maintain neutrality.

Love in the Grand Human Contradiction

Connection in the Toddler brain is illuminated by what the pioneering family theorist, Murray Bowen, described as *emotional fusion*, a process by which parties in a relationship become undifferentiated extensions of each other's feelings. When adults try to love in the Toddler brain, "getting their needs met" means being joined at the hip. Any individual growth or development in one threatens the other.

Toddlers in love assert *autonomy* by rejecting connection, as if they can't have a self without pushing away those they love. They cope with the inherent guilt of rejecting loved ones by finding fault in their partners. The more they perceive that a romantic connection threatens their autonomy, the more fault they find.

Ironically, we lose *ourselves* as we find fault in our partners, and that's the subject of the next chapter.

CHAPTER TWO

How Can I Be Me While You're Being You?

Do you occasionally feel like you become a different person around your partner? Does it seem like he or she has to change—or that you'll have to change partners—for you to be your true self? Do you take turns acting like a stubborn toddler and feeling as powerless as one?

Well, you're not alone. Just about all lovers go through a stage of high emotional reactivity that threatens to destroy their relationship. If one makes a request or an "observation" with any hint of negative emotion, it automatically triggers an unpleasant response in the partner. It doesn't matter how the request and response are worded, the negative emotion underlying them makes both parties feel wronged and like they can't be themselves around each other.

"You're always complaining."

"I'm not complaining, you're criticizing."

"You're so controlling!"

Emotional reactivity is an automatic, usually unconscious response to specific events, situations, or people. Sometimes this is a great thing. While we are falling in love, the mere presence of the beloved fills us with fascination and joy. We thrill at the smiles of our infants and revel in the excitement of new friends. But under stress, emotional reactivity is almost entirely negative. The environment seems more threatening or fraught with uncertainty. Our "buttons get pushed" more easily. We're more likely to lash out or, if we hold it in, emotionally shut down. In couples afflicted with high emotional reactivity, a negative feeling in one partner triggers chaos or shutdown in the other.

All social animals are subject to high emotional reactivity when the environment is perceived to be dangerous. A hair-trigger response shoots adrenaline and cortisol into everyone's bloodstream when one member of the pack senses threat. An alarm in one creates alarm in all, which increases chances of survival; the pack has multiple eyes, ears, and noses and a singular alarm system transmitted from any individual to all the others.

The problem in human intimate relationships is that the Toddler brain is a "better safe than sorry" alarm system. It would rather be wrong 999 times thinking a spouse is a sabertooth tiger than be wrong once thinking a sabertooth tiger is a spouse. Instead of fangs, the partner has an independent will, which is likely to be construed as stubborn or selfish. Behavior requests become demands, calling for submission rather than cooperation, automatically provoking the toddler standoff:

"If you loved me, you'd do this."

"If you loved me, you wouldn't ask me to do this."

One partner's perceived "need" for validation crashes head-long into the "need" of the other not to be controlled. Both end up feeling hurt, angry, and wronged.

High emotional reactivity makes toddler love intolerant of differences (you have to see the world the way I do), narcissistic (incapable of seeing other perspectives), all-or-nothing (you're on a pedestal or you're a demon), and dependent on the current emotional state, which in turn depends on the current physiological state (uncomfortable, tired, hungry, thirsty, overstimulated, or ill). This creates patterns of interacting that make partners seem first like opponents and eventually like enemies.

The Automatic Defense System

Toddler-brain reactivity puts most interactions in the control of an invisible *automatic defense system*. It's invisible because it's most often triggered inadvertently, by body language, facial expressions, tension, distractedness, hesitations, impatience, discomfort, or eagerness. It's activated almost entirely unconsciously; by the time you're aware of any feelings, it's in an advanced stage.

Although the automatic defense system operates in workplace relationships, it does most of its damage in family interactions. Think of your gut reaction when your partner avoids looking at you or merely sighs. Think of how you react when you hear the front door close, even before your partner enters the room or when he or she says something with "that tone," gets that "facial expression," or rolls his or her eyes. Suddenly you find yourself in a defensive posture, prepared for the worst.

When you're both defensive, bad things are likely to happen. All good defense systems have preemptive strike capability. The missiles seem to start flying on their own, with no one giving the order. You find yourself in a battle of cold shoulders, curt exchanges, or hot arguments. You both feel powerless, irritable, impatient, resentful, or angry. You have an impulse to walk away, ignore, criticize, yell, or devalue.

It Gets Hypersensitive!

Sensitivity to the automatic defense system varies throughout the day. There are certain times that are likely to be hair-triggers, which happen to be the times that as toddlers we were the most susceptible to distress: when physical resources are low (tired, hungry, sick), during transitions (stopping one thing, starting another), under stress, or when anxious or feeling down. Over time it grows hypersensitive and stays that way more or less continuously, as we come to expect that our partners will let us down in some way. On the extreme end, it makes us constantly walk on eggshells.

In a later chapter, we'll see how the automatic defense system activates full-blown relationship dynamics that take on a life of their own. When that happens, it seems like you're in a play in which you *must* act out your roles. The topics might change, but the action, characters, and much of the dialogue remain the same.

The Illusion of Sameness

The self-centeredness of the Toddler brain leads us to make one of the biggest mistakes possible in love relationships: assuming that our partners' experience is the same as ours and that events and behaviors mean the same to them as they do to us. I call it the *illusion of sameness.*

In the beginning of relationships, the illusion of sameness allows us to feel some measure of safety in the face of Toddler-brain vulnerability. To ward off the dread of failure (and feelings of inadequacy), we talk ourselves into pleasant delusions:

"Our hearts beat as one."

"We're soul mates."

"We're so close that we complete each other's sentences."

"My partner really believes in me (not projections of me)."

"My partner really *gets* me (not projections of me)."

The illusion of sameness is sometimes disguised in the rhetoric of universal equality; we're all the same, regardless of gender, orientation, race, religion, and so on, as if we marry a gender or race or religion, rather than unique individuals. Universal equality of rights, privilege, and opportunity is a laudable sentiment and a noble social goal that is much abused by those who confuse equality with sameness and who feel uncomfortable with differences. The downside of assuming that we are alike is that I can't accept you, much less love you, unless you think, feel, and behave the way I believe you should.

The price of whatever safety and security we get from the illusion of sameness is an inability to see our partners apart from our feelings about them. As reality changes feelings, as it always does, we get stuck in the Toddler brain, where we blame our partners for each deviation from the illusion we've created. That is, we blame them for being individuals. We blame them for not being us.

There's No "Me-Harmony"

The great irony of the illusion of sameness is that we're most attracted to partners who differ from us. (A copy of yourself dressed up to look like an intimate partner would be so incredibly boring that you might as well live alone.) Besides having different parents, intimate partners are likely to have different core vulnerabilities, different temperaments, different gender socialization, and different support networks. They will certainly have different experiences, different hormones or hormonal levels, and different trajectories to their emotional development. All of these factors will cause them to give different emotional meanings to the same events and experiences. These differences are a large part of what attracts lovers, expands their worldview, and enhances their experience of being alive.

But as early as the second year of living together, couples who love in the wrong part of the brain begin quarreling about the same qualities that attracted them in the first place:

"Yes, in the beginning I loved that you were so energetic. But you don't have to bounce off the damn walls. Just relax!"

"I used to love that you were so calm all the time, but I never bargained for somebody half-dead. Get up and *do* something!"

It's *Not* about "Communication"

Couples whose interactions are dominated by the Toddler brain often fool themselves into thinking their high emotional reactivity—if not all their problems—is rooted in poor communication. Sadly, they find lots of reinforcement for this pervasive myth in pop psychology, where catchy notions that lack empirical support or theoretical validity reign supreme. The great cliché about intimate relationships is that they are all about communication and that communication is all about talking.

First of all, communication is not primarily about talking. We interpret the meaning of spoken words based on the tone of voice, body language, and level of focus/distractedness of both partners. Typically we have an emotional reaction *before* the part of the brain that interprets the meaning of the words is activated. That is, we make a judgment about what is said before we even know the verbal meaning of what is said.

The nonverbal cues that get priority processing in the brain are determined by the motivation of both parties—by what they are trying to do—which is often *not* what they consciously intend to do. If I feel like criticizing but try to hide it with a skillful choice of words, my partner will nevertheless react as if openly criticized. Partners make it worse by arguing about what was said, when they're reacting to the hostility underlying the words that were used.

In intimate relationships, verbal communication is a function of connection, rather than the other way around. When people feel connected, they're able to talk and listen with ease. When they feel disconnected, they tend to attack and counter-attack, however cleverly hidden in verbal skills, as they blame each other for the pain of disconnection. Both partners seem to imply:

"I cannot love you until you agree with me or see things my way or express them the way I think you should."

If partners are motivated to attack or avoid, employing even the most sophisticated communication skills will make them appear phony and manipulative. In my quarter-century of clinical practice, I have never seen skillful communication form a connection without a sincere desire to connect, nor have I seen poor communications skills or choice of words interfere with a sincere desire to connect.

Adults in love don't try to communicate in order to connect. They connect in order to communicate.

Cognitive Dissonance

Most people get married (or otherwise commit to intimate relationships) because they like the way they are with their partners—loving, compassionate, engaging, supportive, sexy, and flexible. They get divorced because they don't like the way they are with their partners—resentful, turned off, frustrated, rigid, or bored, all of which they blame on each other.

Many couples go into joint counseling to find better ways to manipulate their partners into being the way they want (or becoming *who* they want). The self-defeating flaw in this strategy, apart from the fact that it hardly ever works, is *cognitive dissonance*—the discomfort generated by holding contradictory cognitions. In intimate relationships, cognitive dissonance is the difference between how you would like to be and how you are.

"I am loving, compassionate, supportive, and sexy, yet I am not these things with you."

In the Adult brain, cognitive dissonance works as a motivation to be true to your deepest values, by making you behave in more loving and compassionate ways. Unfortunately, most people go to couples therapy in their Toddler brains, where they resolve cognitive dissonance with something like this:

"Since I am unable to be my loving and compassionate self with you, you must be too selfish, insensitive, withholding, demanding, emotional, rigid, sick, or defective in some way."

This ill-fated resolution of cognitive dissonance makes you both feel like victims and sends you searching online or into the self-help aisles of a bookstore for a checklist that validates your suffering and a diagnosis that nails your partner.

Cognitive dissonance undermines intimate relationships (and couples counseling), even when you *are* successful at getting what you want, namely, change in your partner. In that unlikely event, your self-concept is reduced to:

"I am loving, compassionate, and supportive, as long as you do what I want, think like me, and feel the way I do."

If you're reading this book, I know you don't want this on your tombstone:

As long as I got what I wanted, I was great to the people I love.

CHAPTER THREE

Toddler-Brain Coping Mechanisms

C oping mechanisms are adaptations to environmental stress, designed to comfort or give a sense of control. They differ from the old notion of unconscious defense mechanisms, which Freud believed defended the ego from unacceptable impulses, such as sexual feelings for (or hostility toward) parents or caregivers. Coping mechanisms are generally conscious; we're aware that we're blaming, denying responsibility, or avoiding the issue, although we usually begin to do so by habit.

Toddlers use coping mechanisms primarily to ward off threats to autonomy and connection. For example, if you find a toddler alone with a broken toy or lamp and ask what happened, you'll hear, "He/she did it (blame)" or, "I don't know (denial)," or the kid hides or runs away (avoidance). Psychologists used to believe that toddlers used blame, denial, and avoidance merely as attempts to avoid punishment or seek reward. Now we understand that they're also trying, however awkwardly, to maintain some sort of balance between autonomy and connection. After all, the worst thing about punishment to the Toddler brain isn't a time-out or spanking. The deeper pain of punishment is the double-barreled whammy of lost connection and temporary dissolution of the emerging sense of self. When we say "no" to toddlers, as we often must, they perceive it as personal, global, and in no way behavior-specific. It doesn't matter how carefully we try to explain, "You're a good child, but this behavior is wrong." The inchoate sense of self of toddlers cannot distinguish their behaviors from who they are. They require potent (if primitive) coping mechanisms, because almost anything can feel like rejection and self-diminishment.

Most of the time, toddlers can get away with blame, denial, and avoidance because they're so darn cute. When adults do it, we're not so cute.

Adult Blame, Denial, Avoidance

Denial by adults can seem like stubbornness, deception, and insensitivity. It's often those things, too, but it's more centrally an attempt to assert autonomy at the cost of connection:

"Just suck it up, like I do!"

"I don't have to answer to you, just leave me alone!"

Denial can also be used to gain connection at the cost of personal integrity:

"I didn't flirt, I love you!"

"I don't care about visiting my friends, if you don't want me to."

Avoidance is usually indirect, in the form of procrastination, overworking, overdrinking, overeating, overexercising, sexual affairs, and smartphone-mania. When overt, avoidance looks like pouting, sulking, or stonewalling.

Blame is the most insidious of the toddler coping mechanisms employed by adults. It's also the most likely to hijack the Adult brain to justify Toddler-brain splitting—black-and-white, all-good or all-bad perceptions.

Blame is rampant in love relationships (and the culture at large) because it has compelling psychological and social functions. The psychological function is to transfer vulnerable emotional states to someone else. Vulnerable feelings, such as disappointment, sadness, guilt, shame, and anxiety, create self-doubt and make us feel powerless. These can be alleviated with adrenaline, *if* we can blame someone. The adrenaline that powers blame provides temporary feelings of energy and confidence. It also distorts judgment, which is why chronic blamers, in the long run, seem more self-righteous than right.

The temporary energy and confidence of blame comes at a very high price; it ultimately renders us powerless over how we feel. Whomever we blame lives rent-free in our heads, dominating our thoughts, feelings, and behavior, at least for as long as we need the adrenaline. Worse, when we blame our painful emotions on others, they cannot motivate positive changes in behavior or self-concept. Improvement is sacrificed to the impulse to blame and punish.

The social function of blame is to control other people's behavior by invoking guilt or shame in them. Blamers typically struggle with high levels of shame, which they try to transfer to others as often as possible as a means of controlling them, lest they stimulate more guilt and shame. They're prone to imply, if not state overtly: "You should be ashamed of yourself."

The Toddler-brain logic in love relationships is, "If I make you feel unlovable, you'll love me better." The Adult-brain logic is, "We like ourselves better when we're more compassionate and kind."

Blame puts us in the wrong part of the brain and the wrong part of the heart at the wrong time. Blame comes from the alarm-driven Toddler brain, while viable solutions must come from the Adult brain. (Toddlers can't solve problems, they can only set off alarms to get adults to make things better for them.) It comes from the vengeful or retaliatory part of the heart, whereas most of what we blame on loved ones must be addressed from the more humane, compassion-kindness area of our hearts. It locks us in the wrong time dimension with its focus on past causes of problems, whereas solutions must be in the present and future.

Blame traps us in how bad things are. Solutions require ways to make things better.

Blame highlights weaknesses. To help loved ones perform well, we must focus on their strengths and resilience.

Blame blocks effective communication. It makes partners defensive. When defensive, they can't listen to us, no matter how "right" we are.

Blame breeds blame and retaliation. Our blamed partners will find ways to blame us for something, locking us in Toddler-brain standoffs: "It takes one to know one."

Blame, Aggression, and the Grand Human Contradiction

Blame justifies some form of imaginary or overt aggression. When disappointed or hurt, toddlers often become aggressive. They go through a brief developmental stage when they impulsively hit, kick, scratch, bite, pull hair, or otherwise act aggressively. For most children, this is a short-lived behavioral tendency, devoid of ill will or cruelty. Although troubling to many parents, the "aggressive stage" is normal and, managed properly, passes quickly without harm.

The explanation for toddler aggression when I was in doctoral training was that humans are basically uncivilized, so toddlers must be trained in social rules to curtail their aggressive impulses. Thankfully, better research offers a more nuanced interpretation. It turns out that most of the time when toddlers are aggressive, they're trying, however awkwardly and vainly, to balance their competing drives for autonomy and connection. With violent assertions of their autonomy, they try to get others to see their hurt, disappointment, sadness, or frustration. They want compassion! If the parent or sibling who is the object of the aggression gets that the toddler is hurt, disappointed, sad, or frustrated, the connection will become more secure. It's not training in social rules that alters aggressive behavior so much as learning through experience that such behavior is unlikely to garner the compassionate response they really want. When adults get stuck in the Toddler brain, we're likely to hurt each other when we really want compassion, demand submission when we really want cooperation, and insist on "validation" ("My perspective is right and yours is wrong!") when we really want connection.

Some people are aware of the hidden goal of their Toddler-brain aggression:

"I wanted her to know what it feels like to be betrayed. Now we can start over."

"If he doesn't feel really bad, there's no way he'll understand how he hurt me."

But most of the time, there is no intention to hurt. Shame-invoking statements like "You shouldn't be able to look in a mirror, treating me like you do" are *intended* to elicit caring behavior that will strengthen the connection. Instead of reflecting on the behavior and reconceptualizing the intention (Adult-brain activities), we're apt to feel *justified* in continuing to use verbal coercion to make our partners feel bad, in the vain hope that their pain will validate our autonomy and improve the connection.

Toddler brain: "I'm going to make you feel bad until you care about how I feel."

Adult brain: "I want us to focus on our common value—the safe, secure, loving connection we both want."

Ironically, getting people to feel bad for making mistakes in love increases the chances of repeating the mistake. Who is more likely to be loving, compassionate, and kind, the valued self or the devalued self? Who is more likely to blame, deny, and avoid?

Hopefully it is clear from the above that we cannot improve, heal, or grow emotionally while blaming.

Toddler Arguments

Try this experiment: Think of an argument or dispute you had with your significant other. Write down as many exchanges as you can remember. (Better yet, record an argument—as scientists gathering data, not as prosecutors seeking incriminating evidence.) Analyze your statements and those of your partner, and see if you can't reduce the exchanges to one of you saying "Mine!" ("My way!"), and the other saying "No!"

In the Toddler brain, we're keenly aware that our partners don't get our perspectives, with little or no awareness that we're not getting theirs. (Perspective-taking is the province of the Adult brain.) We feel misunderstood and hurt, yet unable to perceive the same feelings in our partners. Instead, we see their superficial reactions to feeling misunderstood and hurt—defensiveness, stubbornness, resentment, or anger—and superficial reactions are all they're likely to see from us.

Toddler-Brain Entitlement

A sense of entitlement is the belief that you have the right to do or get something. In social interactions, it's considering your right to do or get something to be superior to the rights of those who may want to do or get something else. When you feel entitled, you're not merely disappointed when others disagree with you, you feel cheated and wronged, with an impulse to retaliate or seek compensation.

These days most adults feel entitled to "get my needs met" in love relationships. But they're just as likely to resent when their partners act as if they're entitled, calling them selfish, egotistical, or narcissistic. That's another irony of Toddler-brain conflicts; we react negatively to displays of entitlement in our partners but expect full compliance with our own entitlements. It gets to be a downward spiral. The sense of entitlement predicts that we won't get what we think we deserve, which makes us feel even more cheated and entitled to some sort of compensation. The person who cuts in front of you in line is often saying: "With the way I've been treated, I shouldn't have to wait in line, too!"

Entitlement breeds blame and blame breeds more entitlement. The effect on love relationships is to replace "I love you" with "You better meet my needs."

Adults Have Desires and Values

Desires feature more positive motivation than entitlements. If what you desire is based on your deeper values, the act of desiring makes you a better person. For example, the desire to love makes you more lovable, that is, more loving and compassionate.

Desire is appreciative, not entitled; if I desire something I am more likely to appreciate it than if I feel entitled to it. I'll appreciate a bonus for my good work, but I'll demand my contracted salary. I'll appreciate gifts, unless I feel entitled to them. I'll appreciate my partner's help, praise, reward, affection, and support, which I very much want, as long as I don't feel entitled to them because I "need" them.

We'll see how to convert entitlement to desire in Part II of the book. For now, consider this: If you wouldn't drive in a car designed by a toddler or ride in an airplane designed by a toddler, why use coping mechanisms designed by a toddler?

As Toddler-brain coping mechanisms breed entitlement and drain desire, they lead to the destruction of relationships, the topic of our next chapter.

CHAPTER FOUR

Toddler-Brain Relationship Destroyers

The esteemed researcher John Gottman and his associates, in an effort to find predictors of relationship rupture, have observed hundreds of couples in naturalistic interactions. In his research protocol, couples agree to spend a few days in an apartment, which he describes as "the *love lab*, equipped with computers, video cameras, physiological sensors, and an array of fascinating scientific gadgets." Everything they do (except in the bedroom and the bathroom) is recorded and coded for specific behaviors that couples display in routine interactions.

One startling result from his decade-long research is what he calls the "Four Horsemen of the Apocalypse"—criticism, stonewalling, defensiveness, and contempt. Collectively, these self-defeating behaviors predict dissolution of relationships with over 90% accuracy.

It should be noted at the outset that Toddler-brain blame, denial, or avoidance is deeply embedded in the each of the Four Horsemen, which we'll consider separately.

Criticism

Young children have a narrow and rigid view of what is "right" and "fair." Brace for criticism if you divide a cookie between two of them and one gets a crumb more than the other, or if you put their toys in the "wrong" place. When criticism is modeled for them by a parent, sibling, or peer, toddlers are apt to criticize parents and other children, usually in nonverbal ways, such as making faces or noises or throwing something.

Throughout life, the urge to criticize originates in the Toddler brain. (The Adult brain stays focused on improvement.) Adults who retreat to the Toddler brain under stress are likely to be critical in their relationships and see the world in terms of "No!" and "Mine!"

Criticism derives from the toddler coping mechanisms of blame and, to a lesser extent, denial of responsibility. It's the most insidious of the Four Horsemen, as the other three tend to follow from it. When partners feel criticized, they are likely to get defensive, criticize in return, or stonewall. Over time, both the criticized and the criticizers grow contemptuous of each other.

In love relationships, criticism is typically gentle and occasional in the beginning but escalates in due time, becoming hardened and more frequent:

"You and Nordstrom's need a trial separation."

"If you developed some worthwhile interests, you wouldn't have to watch so much TV."

"You're incapable of thinking about anyone but yourself."

"You're such a nag."

"I just read an article that explains why you're such a jerk."
Criticism is destructive to relationships because the
Toddler brain:

- Fills it with blame (rather than solutions)

- Implies there's only one "right way" to do things

- Makes it about personality or character, rather than
  behavior ("You're lazy," rather than, "Could you help
  me with this task?")

- Often makes it belittling ("To belittle, you have to be
  little."—Kahlil Gibran)

The Downward Spiral of Criticism

The criticized person feels controlled, which frustrates the
critical partner, who then steps up the criticism, increasing
the other's sense of being controlled. Both partners can be
aggressive, although the criticized partner is more likely to be
passive-aggressive, agreeing to go along but sabotaging the
agreement down the line:

"You're inconsiderate of my need for a neat and orderly
house."

"Okay, I'll be more considerate."

"Do you mean that, or are you saying that to shut me up?"

"I mean it."

If this dialogue is familiar, you're probably frustrated that
nothing changes. When a partner doesn't follow through on
agreements, the chances are high that he or she feels criticized
much of the time. The internal dialogue—what these partners
say to themselves—goes like this:

"Why follow through on anything?—I'll get criticized no
matter what I do."

"But I have to criticize, or my partner will screw up."

In the Toddler brain, a rather obvious fact never occurs to us: *criticism is an utter failure at getting positive behavior change.* Any short-term compliance we might get from criticism tightens the coil of relationship resentment and motivates some form of payback down the line. For example, if your partner perceives you to be critical, it's more than a little likely that he or she forgets your birthday or anniversary or plays music louder than you prefer or does little things to irritate you. But your partner probably doesn't do those things on purpose. Passive-aggressive behavior is largely unconscious and is motivated to protect the ego rather than defy the criticizer. One of the awful effects of criticism is that criticized partners are likely to lose self-respect and require lots of ego protection.

Of course critical people are smart enough to figure out that criticism doesn't work in love relationships. So why do they keep doing it in the face of mounting frustration and failure?

The answer is simple: Criticism is an easy form of ego defense, and critical people have fragile egos; they tend to be easily insulted and offended. They criticize because they somehow feel *devalued* by their loved ones' behavior or attitudes: "If you don't do what I want, you don't value me." But the perception of being devalued is often inspired by someone simply disagreeing with them.

"Criticism is the only reliable form of autobiography," as Oscar Wilde put it. It tells you more about the psychology of the criticizer than about the people he or she criticizes. Astute professionals can formulate a diagnostic hypothesis just from hearing someone criticize. Frequent criticism often indicates anxiety or depression and almost always low self-value.

Criticism fails in love relationships because it embodies two of the things that most human beings hate the most: It feels like rejection and demands submission. In short, it threatens both autonomy and connection, throwing the Grand Human Contradiction completely out of balance.

Although people hate to submit, we actually like to cooperate, which affords balance of the Grand Human Contradiction. (We *choose* to cooperate, which enhances autonomy, while strengthening the connection.) We have a built-in reward of well-being for cooperation, probably because it was necessary for the survival of the species. Critical people demand submission but they really want cooperation—willing, resentment-free behaviors to further the good of the relationship. They seem oblivious to this key point about human nature: *The valued self cooperates; the devalued self resists.*

If you want behavior change from a partner, child, relative, or friend, first show value for that person. If you want resistance, criticize.

The Roots of Criticism

Believe it or not, the roots of criticism have to do with survival.

Critical people were often criticized in early childhood by caretakers, siblings, or peers, at an age when criticism can be especially painful. Young children cannot distinguish criticism of their behavior from outright rejection, no matter how much we try to make the distinction for them, as in the well-intentioned "You're a good boy, but this behavior is bad." Such a distinction requires a higher prefrontal cortex operation beyond the neural capacity of young children. For a child under seven, anything more than very occasional criticism, even if soft-pedaled or sugar-coated, means they're not good enough.

So what does this have to do with survival? Well, the only thing young children can do to survive is attach emotionally to people who will take care of them. Feeling unworthy of attachment, as criticized young children are apt to feel, can seem like life or death. So they try to control the great pain of criticism by turning it into *self*-criticism. Self-inflicted pain is better than unpredictable rejection by loved ones.

By early adolescence, criticized children begin to "identify with the aggressor" and emulate the seemingly more powerful criticizer. As a result, they expand their self-criticism to criticism of others. By young adulthood, they appear to have shifted entirely to criticism of others, as they try to control other people's behavior by re-creating in them the feelings of inadequacy and unworthiness they felt as criticized children.

Most critical adults remain primarily self-critical. (I have never treated one who was not.) As hard as they are on others, they're at least equally hard on themselves.

How to Tell If You're Critical

A hallmark of critical people is that, like toddlers, they hate to be criticized themselves. If you react to the most mild criticism or disagreement with anger and an impulse to retaliate, you're probably critical of other people. This is more complicated than simply being able to "dish it out but not take it." Criticizing others is the primary coping mechanism of critical people. When criticism is turned on them, it exposes injuries that can date as far back as toddlerhood and automatically invoke the toddler coping mechanisms

In intimate relationships, you're likely to be the last to know that you're critical. We tend to whitewash in ourselves those qualities we find negative in others. (As the joke goes, "I give feedback; you're critical. I'm firm; you're stubborn. I'm flexible; you're wishy-washy. I'm in touch with my feelings; you're hysterical! I'm reasonable, you're cold and calculating.") In general, if your partner is defensive or says that you're critical, it's a pretty good bet that you are. But there's another way to tell, by noticing your automatic thoughts.

Think of what you automatically say to yourself if you drop something or make a mistake. Critical people will typically think, "Oh you idiot," or, "jerk," or just curse or sigh in disappointment or disgust with themselves. When you make a more serious mistake, self-reproach and self-criticism are likely to turn caustic. If you do these things to yourself, you most likely do them to others.

Criticism (Toddler Brain) vs. Feedback (Adult Brain)

Critical people often delude themselves into thinking that they merely give helpful feedback. In fairness, there is sometimes an overlap. The following are ways to tell the two apart.

Criticism focuses on what's wrong. (Why can't you pay attention to the bills?)

Feedback focuses on how to improve. (Let's go over the bills together.)

Criticism implies the worst about the other's personality. (You're stubborn and lazy.)

Feedback is about behavior, not personality. (Can we start by sorting the bills according to the due date?)

Criticism devalues. (You're just not smart enough to do this, or you're too unreliable, stubborn, selfish, immoral, and so on.)

Feedback encourages. (I know you have a lot on your plate, but I'm pretty sure we can do this together.)

Criticism implies past blame. (It's your fault we're in this financial mess.)

Feedback focuses on future improvement. (We can get out of this mess if we both give up a few things.)

Criticism attempts to control. (You have to do what I say because I'm smarter, more educated, more moral, and so on.)

Feedback respects autonomy. (Of course you have the right to make that choice, but it doesn't really work for me. Is there something else we can do?)

Criticism is coercive. (You're going to do what I want, or else I won't connect with you or will punish you in some way.)

Feedback is cooperative. (I know we can find a solution that works for both of us.)

A Warning About Feedback

If you're angry or resentful, any "feedback" you give will be heard as criticism, no matter how you put it. That's because people respond to emotional tone, not intention, and the emotional tone of anger and resentment always devalues, and often warns, threatens, and intimidates. Regulate anger or resentment before you try to give feedback. We give feedback in the Adult brain, *after* we regulate Toddler-brain impulses to criticize. To give feedback, focus on how to improve and on the behavior you would like to see, not on your partner's personality. Encourage change, instead of undermining confidence. Sincerely offer help. Respect autonomy. Resist the urge to punish or pout.

The key to shifting from Toddler-brain criticism to Adult-brain feedback is to focus on what we want—improvement—rather than what we don't want, which is whatever we feel like criticizing. Once in the Adult brain, we're more aware of the effect of the criticism on the loved one, which is entirely negative and counterproductive.

If you're a critical person, you must absolutely get a handle on your impulse to criticize, before it ruins your relationship. Criticism is to the vibrancy of your relationship what smoking is to your health.

Stonewalling

Stonewalling derives from the toddler coping mechanism of avoidance. Toddlers pout; adults in the Toddler brain stonewall. This is not to be confused with the occasional "time-out" to calm down or collect your thoughts. Stonewalling is an absolute refusal to consider your partner's perspective. If you listen at all, you do it dismissively or contemptuously. The common songs of the stonewaller are:

"Just leave me alone . . ."

"Do whatever you want . . ."

"End of conversation . . ."

"Stop talking . . ."

"Get out of my face . . ."

"That's enough . . ."

"I've had it!"

The other divorce-predictive behaviors (criticism, defensiveness, and contempt) are gender neutral, that is, men and women do them more or less equally. Stonewalling, according to the research of Gottman and others, as well as the experience of most couples counselors, is far more likely to be a male thing. When women stonewall, it's typically a function of temperament; they're shy, inhibited, or introverted. More commonly for women, it's a learned behavior. Engaging in conflict or emotion-laden conversation has exposed them to put-downs or abuse in the past. Of course, cultural reinforcement plays a large part, as the icon of the "strong, silent male," reinforces stonewalling as a relationship tactic.

Aggressive vs. Defensive Stonewalls

In aggressive stonewalling the stonewaller knows he's hurting his partner with silence, cold shoulders, and emotional isolation. He stonewalls to gain leverage or power. This is a common tactic in battering relationships, in which the more powerful partner systematically tries to control or dominate the less powerful one. If you're in an abusive relationship, nothing you try to do unilaterally will guarantee your safety. Here's the best you can do:

"It hurts me when you shut me out, and I know you don't want to hurt me."

If your partner doesn't care that you're hurt, the relationship is not safe and is more likely to worsen than improve. It will do more harm than good. (For help with emotional abuse, see the website compassionpower.com. If physical abuse occurs, seek help from your local domestic violence organization.)

In the more common defensive version of stonewalling, conflict seems overwhelming to stonewallers. Their only choice in the Toddler brain is to hide behind a stone wall.

It Looks Different on the Outside

While stonewalling can look aggressive, mean, or childish from the outside, it feels very different on the inside. The defensive stonewaller feels like he's trying to protect himself. He can also think that he's protecting his family. Not only have I observed this countless times in my clients; there was a time when I experienced it in my personal life. For about 10 years or so, before becoming a therapist, I regularly stonewalled my wife when things got tough. I was afraid of my anger, having grown up in a severely violent home. I never wanted my wife or daughter to see that kind of rage or know that kind of chaos. In truth, I never had much anger, but there was always the fear.

We stonewall to avoid feeling inadequate. We're convinced that we'll fail to improve matters if we try to engage—fail as communicators and, more important, as protectors. But like all avoidance strategies, stonewalling reinforces the false perception of the self as inadequate and unlovable, or else we wouldn't "need" to do it. Thus the more we do it, the more it seems that we have to do it.

Men are less likely than women to know when they stonewall, because it seems so natural for them. Little boys turn pouting into stonewalling at as early as four or five years old. A sure sign that you're a stonewaller is the belief that your partner nags you. That means you're not listening. A nagging partner is an unheard partner.

If you're a stonewaller, you must become aware of the hurtful effects of the behavior on your partner, who will not be able to tell the difference between aggressive and defensive stonewalling. To save your relationship, you must give up blame, denial, and avoidance, and replace them with the Adult-brain coping mechanisms: *improve*, *appreciate*, *connect*, and *protect*. Part II will show how.

Steven Stosny

Defensiveness

Defensiveness derives from the toddler coping mechanism of denial. Toddlers do it in the sing-song, *"I don't know."* Adults in the Toddler brain do it primarily through deflection (changing the subject or deliberately misinterpreting), excuse-making, and outright deceit.

I have to admit to being a little surprised when research identified defensiveness as a leading predictor of divorce. I was trained as a therapist to regard the defensiveness of a client as a signal that I was coming off too strongly or too judgmentally. So I assumed that when my clients were defensive, they were perceiving accusation. The solution for couples seemed obvious; train them to speak without accusation and the defensiveness would go away. That naïve belief proved way too simple.

Defensiveness damages relationships because it dismisses partners' concerns and invalidates or minimizes their hurt: "You have no right to be concerned or hurt, because I'm right, (or because) I had no intention to hurt you."

Defensiveness often takes the form of counter-accusations, such as:

"I never said that, you misheard."

"I might have said that *after* you said *this*!"

"What about when you did something worse?"

"There you go, another pity party, you're the only one who's inconvenienced."

"Just let it go and let's move on!"

Contempt

Contempt employs all the toddler coping mechanisms: blame, denial, and avoidance. In love relationships, contempt occurs at the end of a long chain of resentment—accumulated perceptions of unfairness, of not getting the help, appreciation, consideration, praise, reward, or affection we think we deserve. As the chain grows ever more links (of things we resent), our partners seem more like opponents than loved ones. We see the problem not in the way we interact or regulate emotions. Rather, the problem is the *character* of our partners. We view them as immoral, selfish, unstable, or stupid—there's *something wrong* with them. Contempt sends people to the Internet to diagnose their partners with various personality disorders.

Unfortunately, few Internet sites warn that differential diagnosis of personality disorders is extremely complex and should be supported by psychological testing. They don't mention that even highly trained professionals cannot validly diagnose loved ones with personality disorders, and it is unethical for them to pretend that they have the objectivity to do so.

But whether or not the "diagnosis" of a loved one is accurate is really immaterial. The desire to diagnose a partner typically indicates a level of contempt that, unabated, spells doom for the relationship. It's hard to be compassionate, kind, and loving to someone you hold in contempt, and it's equally hard to be compassionate, kind, and loving to someone who holds you in contempt. A relationship in contempt is like a patient on life support. Without heroic intervention, it will die.

How to Know That You Have Contempt for Your Partner
Contempt is present when you use (or at least think) contemptuous attributions such as: "You're lazy, selfish, inconsiderate, crazy, narcissistic, borderline . . ." and so on.

Typically, such negative labels reinforce the kind of behavior you *don't* want, and almost guarantee that you'll get more of it. After all, what do lazy, selfish, inconsiderate, and crazy people do? Or *don't* do? Contempt is the ultimate in self-fulfilling prophecy. That's because contemptuous attributions eliminate all chance of improvement. The negatively labeled partner (or child) inevitably gives up. It's unclear, for example, how many helpful and considerate things you have to do not to be considered lazy, selfish, and inconsiderate anymore. Worst of all, the partner or child burdened with negative labels comes to identify with them. As one teenage client put it:

"All my life they've been telling me I'm a bad kid. Why don't they just back off and let me do my job?"

Why It Gets Worse

If you're getting more and more of the behavior you don't want, it's a pretty safe bet that you have contempt for your partner. Please understand, I'm not saying that your contempt caused things to get bad. But you must also understand that contempt keeps them from getting better, due to a phenomenon known as *projective identification.*

Projection is what we do when we attribute our own emotional states, attitudes, or expectations to others. When partners feel irritable, for instance, they often accuse their partners of being irritable, too. If one partner feels guilty about his attraction to an actress on TV, he might say that his partner ogles the leading man. Partners who expect to be disappointed or mistreated project that interpretation onto just about everything their partners feel and do.

Projective identification occurs when we identify with the projection—you get irritable when your partner accuses you of being irritable, and you notice how hot the movie star is, once your partner mentions it. Similarly, children can easily identify with adult projections about them being "bad, naughty, selfish, lazy," and so on.

Projective identification happens so often in daily living that we hardly notice it. If a girlfriend believes that you gossip about her, you have an urge to let another girlfriend know that she feels that way. If someone believes you don't like him, you start to notice things about him that you really don't like. If you have coworkers or acquaintances who think you have a good sense of humor, you try to be funny around them. Those who think you're compassionate inspire you to go out of your way to inquire about the well-being of their children. If some people think you're intelligent, you try not to say anything dumb around them. If someone thinks you're critical, you'll feel an urge to criticize. And if some people think you're selfish, you're not likely to express concern about their health and happiness.

Of course we don't have to conform to people's projections, but it requires conscious attention not to; on autopilot, projective identification usually prevails. The probable reason that projective identification is so strong is that it enables us to predict behavior in social contexts, which is necessary for a sense of safety and order. Unpredictable behavior stirs anxiety, as when someone speaks loudly in a restaurant, undresses in public, or says impolite things at a dinner party.

Contempt as a Defense

Once contempt becomes part of a person's defense system, change in the partner's behavior will not alter it. The partner's behavior may have started it, but once it has started, contempt takes on a life of its own when embedded in the perceptions of the person who drags it through life. I have never seen a case where behavior change by one partner alone altered the other partner's contempt. Even if the offending partner does everything the aggrieved partner wants, there will be resentment that it didn't happen sooner:

"All those years I wasted with you being a selfish jerk, and *now* you decide to be nice!"

As long as contempt persists, any positive behavior change by one partner will seem like too little, too late.

Contempt Makes You Contemptuous

The first thing you need to know about contempt is that it affects you more negatively than it does anyone else. It's impossible to like yourself as much as you deserve *while* you feel contempt. Although aimed at your partner, it's filled with hidden self-anger and self-contempt for "putting up with it." You'll likely beat yourself up for trusting or believing your partner in the first place.

In addition to its psychological detriments, contempt lowers the efficiency of your immune system and often causes minor physical ailments, exhaustion, coughs, colds, aches, and pains. You'll never feel quite okay as long as you hold contempt.

Contempt Is Contagious

Contempt is extremely contagious and highly influenced by projection. If you're around a contemptuous person, you're likely to become more contemptuous. If you project contemptuous characterizations onto someone, such as "loser, abuser, selfish, lazy, narcissistic, irrational, devious," they're likely to conform to your projections.

Because contempt in a relationship is so contagious, the toddler standoff sounds like this:

"I'll stop being irritable when you stop being selfish."

"I'll stop being selfish when you stop being irritable."

Compassion is also contagious, albeit to a lesser extent. If you're around a compassionate person, you're likely to become more compassionate, and if you project onto people that they're compassionate, they're likely to become more thoughtful of others.

In Part II, we'll see how to use projective identification to your advantage.

Beware of Being Right

When adults retreat to the Toddler brain under stress, they suffer the toddler curse: a persistent need to be right. It's a curse because it drains relationships of compassion:

"I don't care that you're hurt because you're wrong."

Seeming to be right justifies criticism, stonewalling, defensiveness, contempt, and even the destruction of relationships.

The Toddler-brain "need" to be right creates an *illusion of certainty*.

A perception of certainty is illusory because it's an emotional state, not an intellectual one. To create a feeling of certainty, the brain must filter out far more information than it processes, increasing its already high error rate during emotional arousal. In other words, the more certain we feel when emotionally aroused, the more likely it is that we're wrong in important ways. Neurologist Robert A. Burton has an excellent book on the subject: *On Being Certain: Believing You Are Right Even When You're Not.*

High-adrenaline emotions, particularly anger and fear, create the profoundest illusions of certainty, due to their amphetamine effects. Amphetamines, like adrenaline, create a temporary sense of confidence and energy, making you feel like you can do anything. But they achieve feelings of confidence by narrowing mental focus and eliminating most variables from consideration. That's why you feel more confident after a cup of coffee (a mild amphetamine effect) than before it. It's why you're certain of danger when you're afraid, that you're a failure or defective when you're ashamed, and that you're right—and everyone else is wrong—when you're angry.

Bottom line: It's never enough to be right, even if you are. The ultimate measure of love relationships is compassion and kindness. When those fail, it doesn't matter who's right. When you fail at compassion and kindness in love, you're wrong even when you're factually right.

Another kind of relationship destroyer that plagues adults who retreat to the Toddler brain under stress is *jealousy*, the topic of our next chapter.

CHAPTER FIVE

Toddler Love Is a Jealous God

No emotional state keeps us stuck in the Toddler brain as relentlessly and as mercilessly as the "green-eyed monster." Few emotional states engender as much confusion and passion. Yet jealousy is natural and can be harmless, even beneficial to a relationship, in very small doses. To understand how, we have to distinguish simple jealousy from its more complex versions.

Simple jealousy is a universal experience. It starts as a feeling of discomfort at the prospect of losing reward or affection to someone else. It first emerges in toddlerhood, typically when the child witnesses parents showing affection to each other or to another child. The toddler at first squeezes between the embracing adults and tries to be as cute and lovable as possible. Similarly, the arrival of a sibling often causes regression to things like bedwetting and less mature speech. The regression is, in part, the child's attempt to seem more lovable to the distracted parents:

"Babies turn you on? I can do that, too!"

In general, simple jealousy motivates reward-seeking behavior; you try to be more cooperative, helpful, or loving.

That usually gets a positive response, which is sufficient to alleviate the discomfort of jealousy.

Simple jealousy functions as a kind of distance regulator in close relationships. When loved ones drift apart, the pang of jealousy motivates more attention and connecting behavior, similar to the toddler squeezing between the embracing parents. It occurs more frequently when the relationship is most insecure, particularly in the early stages of emotional bonding, when the parties feel the most vulnerable to rejection. It goes largely unnoticed at that time, because the partners follow its natural motivation to be more loving. They reconnect, and the jealousy immediately recedes.

Many people use low-level simple jealousy to test the affections of their prospective partners. One might look in the eyes of the waiter as he places the coffee on the table, just to see how her date will respond. Another might joke with the waitress as she takes their order. A little discomfort exhibited by the potential partner makes them feel safe enough to invest in the relationship. The jealousy is barely noticed because they follow its motivation to close the distance between them.

When the parties cannot or will not reconnect, simple jealousy fails to function. Once resentment takes over the relationship and systematically blocks emotional connection, simple jealousy fades into more generalized negative feelings for each other. It's not a good sign when resentment replaces simple jealousy. Contempt will soon follow.

In *complex* jealousy, the prospect of loss feels like punishment, making you feel smaller, less valuable, and more powerless. It has a built-in retaliation motive, which often leads to some sort of attack, usually verbal, either overt or imaginary. Toddlers have been known to throw things at infant siblings and harm pets who seem to take away the affection of parents.

The development of complex jealousy coincides with the emerging sense of self in late toddlerhood. It grows full-blown in adolescence and, by early adulthood, poses a major problem in close relationships for those who retreat to the Toddler brain under stress. The hallmark of complex jealousy is obsession— you can't stop thinking about incidents, real or imagined, that invoke it.

Obsessions make thoughts race by, only to loop back again in an endless cycle. The faster they go and the more frequently they recur, the less accurate they become as assessments of reality. A lover's friendly smile at someone else turns into full-blown intercourse in a turbulent imagination. If the obsessions persist, they take on paranoid, delusional, or hallucinatory characteristics.

I remember one court-ordered client, whom I'll call Fred, whose jealousy was so threatening that his wife locked herself and their 10-year-old daughter in the bedroom. Fred was convinced that he heard sounds of his wife having sex with another man behind the closed door, despite his wife and little girl crying in fear and anguish. He heard his daughter wailing, "Daddy, please, there's nobody here but us!" Yet the auditory hallucination—the sounds of lovemaking—persisted in his head, even after the police arrived to subdue him.

Fred's degree of obsessive jealousy, like the tragic and all-too-frequent cases of murder-suicide of intimate partners, is extreme and, thankfully, rare. (If you ever fear for your safety in a relationship, or if your partner violates personal boundaries, seek help from your local domestic violence organization.) Nevertheless, love in the Toddler brain tends to be possessive, controlling, and sometimes dangerous. Indeed, all abusive impulses originate in the Toddler brain. As lovable as toddlers are, adults who love like toddlers are the stuff of relationship nightmares.

Because it rises and falls on the ebb and flow of feelings, complex jealousy has a Jekyll and Hyde quality. When the afflicted feel close to their partners, they're at a loss as to why they ever felt jealous: "How could I have thought those ugly things?" or, "He's so wonderful, how could I ever imagine he'd betray me?" Once the feelings of closeness ebb, the obsessions crash back, making jealous partners feel and act like completely different people. If you've been accused of having a Jekyll and Hyde personality in a love relationship, complex jealousy is a likely reason.

Simple Jealousy Can Get Complicated

Simple jealousy can easily turn complex. If the child squeezing between the embracing parents is pushed away or accused of being selfish, he or she may then interpret the discomfort of exclusion not as an internal motivation to connect, but as external attack, prompting an impulse to retaliate. Punishing children for jealousy drives the feelings underground, where they grow insidiously powerful. Adults who were punished as children for feeling simple jealousy—that is, who were made to feel unlovable for wanting to be loved—are likely to direct a great deal of anger toward loved ones when trapped in the Toddler brain.

Simple jealousy can seem complicated when the parties are insensitive to each other's different personality traits and temperamental qualities. For instance, an introvert is likely to resent an extroverted partner's notion of "appropriate behavior" with perceived rivals. What is honest "friendliness" for one seems "flirtatious" to the other. What sincerely feels like "consideration" to one—*You should show me respect by not talking to him/her*—honestly feels like "control" or even "oppression" to the other—*You don't want me to be myself.*

This is still simple jealousy, without the paranoid or obsessional characteristics of its darker cousin. The introverted partner is neither alleging infidelity nor obsessing about the possibility. It's really a classic temperamental error that occurs in most relationships: judging your partner by how you would react, even though your partner has a different temperament, different experiences, and different developmental and emotional history.

For example, if the more introverted partner were to speak with interest to someone at a party, it might well mean that he or she is flirting. The error is assuming that the same behavior— talking with interest—has the same meaning (flirtation) for the extroverted partner, which is probably untrue. We're all tempted to judge our partners by what we would do in similar circumstances. But it's really a form of Toddler-brain self-centeredness—the way *I* would behave is the standard for all decent people, so you must conform to what I think is appropriate.

Create Value or Drive Yourself Crazy

Simple jealousy raises the value of the loved one—you want more of him or her and generally appreciate what you get. A little bit of simple jealousy is actually good for a relationship. Most people would not want a lover who couldn't care less if they slept with everyone on the hockey team. But even simple jealousy must be limited to small doses. Think of it as a concentrated acid that needs lots of dilution to be effective without doing harm.

Complex jealousy devalues the loved one—you want to punish, avoid, or control. It never comes in small doses and eventually eats through the heart of the relationship.

In the Toddler brain, jealousy is "the green-eyed monster that mocks the flesh it doth eat," as Shakespeare put it. It cuts us off from the ability to create value and meaning in life. It keeps us isolated in our obsessions. By making an enemy of the beloved, it devours the relationship, leaving a skeleton of resentment and hostility.

Disarming the jealousy complex can only be done in the Adult brain, as we'll learn to do in Part II.

CHAPTER SIX

Relationship Dynamics in Toddler Love

As we've seen, the toddler coping mechanisms of blame, denial, and avoidance make us prone to criticism, stonewalling, defensiveness, and contempt, which eventually destroy relationships. They also lead inevitably to the development of various *intimate relationship dynamics.*

If you and your partner have the same dialogues, disagreements, or arguments over and over, it's probably the work of an intimate relationship dynamic fueled by the noisome alarms of the Toddler brain. Intimate relationship dynamics are interactive patterns in which both parties automatically react to each other in set ways. In the throes of the dynamic, partners are keenly sensitive to how "the other" behaves but scarcely aware of their own behavior. They know painfully well that they're reacting to their partners' "cold" or "unreasonable" (or worse) attitudes. Yet they have no idea of what their cold or unreasonable (or worse) partners are reacting *to* or how their partners perceive *them* at the moment of the interaction.

It's not so much that individuals are in denial of their role in the dynamic. Nor are one or both partners necessarily devious or manipulative, although they can seem that way as the dynamic takes over the relationship. The deeper problem is that it's extremely difficult to objectively analyze one's own behavior. Only a tiny sliver of the prefrontal cortex serves that purpose, and it gets practically no blood during emotional arousal. Think of when you *are* able to objectively analyze your own behavior. You practically need a weekend retreat away from all distractions to access that ability, which is exclusive to the Adult brain.

Just in case the inability to objectively analyze our own behavior isn't bad enough, consider the fact that the worst thing your partner says or does goes into long-term memory, while the worst thing *you* do or say does not. You'll remember the worst thing your partner said or did, probably with a great deal of accuracy, but you'll recall with far less accuracy your part of the exchanges leading up to it.

"I can't believe you said that to me last night."

"I didn't say that to you, you said this to me."

"*If* I said this, it was after you said that."

"No, *if* I said that, it was *after* you said this."

They'll never convince each other, because natural selection happened to favor recording the injuries we suffer over those we inflict. The critical partner accuses the stonewaller of defensiveness and the stonewaller views the critical partner as nagging. The aggressive one is convinced that the withdrawer is passive-aggressive; the avoider is sure that the pursuing partner is smothering.

Once emotional arousal subsides, the self-analytical part of the prefrontal cortex partially reengages, often with a torrent of self-doubt. In the beginning of a relationship, self-doubt prompts guilt and remorse, which motivate reconnection—you kiss and make up.

Over time self-doubt and guilt are processed predominantly in the Toddler brain, where they will likely be blamed on the partner and give way to chronic resentment. Eventually, the negative feelings of both partners are attributed not to the dynamic between them, but to some flaw in the other's character.

Nobody Starts It, and It Doesn't Matter What It's About

Intimate relationship dynamics can swing into full force with neither party doing anything wrong. They're activated by the automatic defense system (discussed in Chapter Two), which in turn is triggered mostly by nonverbal cues, such as body language, tone of voice, distraction, eye contact (or aversion), disparate energy levels, and unconscious projections. Once an intimate relationship dynamic is activated, the content of the exchange—what the discussion or argument is about—whether serious or trivial, simply doesn't matter; the parties slip into their habitual reactions, no matter what.

The major unconscious dynamics of Toddler-brain relationships are *demand-withdraw*, *pursuer-distancer*, and *fear-shame*.

Demand-Withdraw

The *demand-withdraw* dynamic is mainly about power: who will control whom. One party seeks control through criticism, complaints, or coercion, while the other controls through distraction or isolation. One partner is aggressive while the other is likely to be passive-aggressive. The dialogue is essentially a toddler standoff, with one saying, "Mine!" (or "My way!") and the other saying, "No!"

Drake insists that Eva spends too much money and evades her share of the household chores. Believing that nothing she does is good enough for him, Eva has made progressively less effort to nurture the relationship and help around the house, prompting ever more demands from her partner. Occasionally she "feels cornered" and lashes out with a surge of verbal abuse.

"You *....ing *...hole! You need to do housework, 'cause you're not a real man. Who on earth could be romantic to you, the way you treat people?"

It's common in the demand-withdraw dynamic that both parties feel like victims and see their partners as abusers.

The demander sees the "issue" as the withdrawer's laziness, selfishness, obstinacy, or sabotage. The withdrawer sees the issue as the demander's need to control and general lack of empathy.

For example, Sylvie believes the primary issue of her marriage is her husband's continually lying to her. She cites as an example the time he told her that he had paid the insurance bill on time when he actually paid it past due, along with a penalty. From Frank's perspective, the only issue was the fact that he *couldn't* tell her about his mistake, because it would begin "an onslaught of criticism that would last all night."

They fought all night anyway, about his "lying and lack of integrity" and her "criticism and need to control everything," with each citing numerous examples of the other's failings. In advanced stages, demand-withdraw seems more like *prosecution-defense*, with both sides painting the worst possible picture of each other.

Neither partner could see that it was really the demand-withdraw dynamic making them play out endless Toddler-brain interactions: Sylvie constantly looked for something Frank might do to raise her anxiety (so it didn't "sneak up" on her), while he just as persistently tried to hide things from her to avoid shaming criticism. Their interactive dynamic was the core problem, a product of the blame, denial, and avoidance they used to cope with their vulnerable emotions.

Reversal at the End

Demanders eventually give up, out of exhaustion (it takes more emotional energy to demand than to withdraw), resignation, despair, or bitter contempt. Sensing that it is safe to voice some of their own demands, former withdrawers start demanding with a vengeance, prompting their partners to disengage.

Melvin confronts his wife, Anna, with "insights" he got from his therapist: "All these years I thought I was just tired [his excuse for avoidance], but I'm really neglected, burdened, unappreciated, mistreated, and taken advantage of."

Not surprisingly, his complaints were virtually identical to Anna's when she was the demander, before she gave up on the relationship. That's because they lost the heart of their relationship in the tension of their dynamic. They lost sight of what they both wanted to give and receive—value, respect, and cooperation. In the Toddler brain, one demands while the other withdraws, and no one freely gives or receives what they want.

Pursuer-Distancer

A close cousin of demand-withdraw is the *pursuer-distancer* dynamic. More about connection than power, the dance of pursuer-distancer has one party trying to achieve a degree of closeness and intimacy considered by the other to be smothering. Any attempt by the pursuer to get more closeness is met with resistance and more distance.

There are many ways of creating distance in intimate relationships. The most common are workaholism (or other obsessions); over-involvement with children, friends, or neighbors; pornography; and affairs.

Pursuers can be creative in attempts to engineer closeness, while distancers can be just as fervent in their resistance. For example, Sheila got her husband to agree to a weekend in the mountains with their best friends. Harry was furious when they got to the cabin only to find that the other couple had canceled at the last minute. He called the husband of the other couple, who knew nothing about the proposed weekend.

Feeling controlled and manipulated, Harry threatened to leave Sheila in the cabin alone. He ended up staying the whole weekend but barely spoke to her. When he saw her crying several times during those long two days together, he tried to explain that he had to be firm: "I can't let your manipulation harm our relationship."

Sheila's ruse to lure her husband into a romantic interlude never had a chance in the throes of their Toddler-brain dynamic. *Every pursuer-distancer sequence ends in some form of rejection of the pursuer.*

Pursuers see the primary relationship issue as the coldness and withholding nature of their partners:

"You just throw me a few crumbs of affection now and then. You don't care at all about my needs."

Distancers see the "issue" as the neediness of their partners:

"Nothing I do is enough for you. Nobody could meet your needs."

The accumulated guilt from rejecting a loved one—and the shame of being rejected *by* a loved one—activate cycles of resentment, anger, and hostility that drain the life from relationships.

Reversal at the End

A reversal of roles occurs near the end of pursuer-distancer relationships, just as it does in the demand-withdraw dynamic. Pursuers eventually stop pursuing when the weight of continual rejection becomes too great. They make less eye contact, close off their body language, and appear tired, irritable, cynical, or angry much of the time. The cessation of pursuit makes distancers unsure of who they are, because a cornerstone of their identity is the unbridled devotion of the pursuer. In desperation, they start their own pursuit of the weary, angry, or numb former pursuer, in large part to retrieve the cornerstone of their identities. Distancers tend to fall in love with their partners as, bags in hand, they finally walk out the door.

Fear-Shame

The most pervasive and hardest to detect of intimate relationship dynamics, the *fear-shame* dynamic is deeply embedded in the other two. In this particularly insidious pattern of automatic behavior, fear in one partner stimulates shame in the other and vice versa. Actually, it's more accurate to say that partners react to each other's ways of *avoiding* fear and shame. Both are so loathsome and painful that most adults have forged entrenched habits of toddler coping mechanisms to elude experiencing them.

Fear-avoidant behavior in one partner triggers shame-avoidant behavior (expressed as withdrawal or aggression) in the other, and vice versa. One frets or worries; the other shuts down or gets angry. One gets angry, resentful, or quiet; the other worries or feels isolated. In the Toddler brain, both blame their feelings on each other.

Steven Stosny

Fear, Shame, and Hormones

Fear-shame, unlike the pursuer-distancer and demand-withdraw dynamics, is greatly influenced by hormones. On a day-to-day basis, the activation of various habits of avoiding fear and shame owes largely to the effects of dominant hormones. Estrogen enhances fear. Relative to higher-testosterone people, higher-estrogen folks have a lower threshold of fear, stay in it longer, and often have flashbacks of events that stimulated fear. Estrogen also drives nest-making (decorating the home) and alliance-building (nurturing friendships), probably because there's safety in numbers and security in nests.

Testosterone blunts fear and drives competitiveness and status-seeking, while increasing dread of failure and loss of status. Relative to high-estrogen people, those with high testosterone have a lower threshold of shame and, when they fail to avoid it, they stay in it much longer and experience flashbacks of humiliation.

Although these hormones are present in all social animals, their effects are of course more complicated in humans. We've confounded the production and balance of hormones by ranging all over the planet (climate affects hormone production), not sleeping in real darkness (hormones are partially replenished in darkness), taking a variety of medications, eating lots of animals that are rather alarmingly overdosed with hormones, and experiencing rapid societal changes in competitiveness and hierarchy. It's perfectly normal in humans (and more interesting) to have high-testosterone girls and women, high-estrogen boys and men, and a rich mixture of both hormones in either sex.

It seems to be an element of attraction that, in general, high-testosterone and high-estrogen potential partners are drawn to each other, regardless of sex, sexual assignment, or sexual orientation. Differences in reactions to fear and shame exist in virtually all love relationships.

Survival

The fear-shame dynamic is a survival-based mechanism observed in most social animals. The females tend to be more fearful and vigilant than the males in general, but especially when they have young. They also tend to have better hearing and/or sense of smell, making them ideal alarm systems for the group. Males are larger, more powerful, more aggressive, and more expendable (the pack will have billions of sperm but only a handful of eggs). The anatomy of males makes them better suited to protect against intruders and predators. Males who fail to respond to female fear with protective aggression are subject to attack by more dominant males. Though anthropomorphizing is risky, the failure to protect causes a vulnerability in the males of social animals that seems close to what we would call shame.

The human brain is more socially structured than that of any other animal. In us, the fear-shame dynamic takes on more complicated forms that undermine intimate relationships. Confronted with the anxiety or fear of higher-estrogen partners, higher-testosterone partners instinctively respond with protection or support. But if they don't know how to protect or support—or can only remember failures to support or protect—they're likely to employ one of two defensive strategies. They either turn the aggression onto their partners (usually in the form of criticism, "superior reasoning," controlling behavior, coercion, and so on), or they'll rein in aggressive impulses by withdrawing (stonewalling or "going quiet"). Anger or withdrawal by higher-testosterone partners stimulates anxiety or fear of isolation in higher-estrogen partners, even if the anger or withdrawal has nothing to do with the anxious partners. (By the way, *fear of isolation* is not the same as loneliness. Fear of isolation is the sense that no one cares about you. Most high-estrogen people don't mind being alone, as long as they don't feel isolated.)

A common example of the fear-shame dynamic occurs on the highway. When higher-estrogen passengers are startled, high-testosterone drivers get angry, perceiving the response as an assault on their charioteering. They'll sulk or say something sarcastic or turn into Ben-Hur, ready to drive those other chariots off the road. Any of the above makes passengers more anxious or afraid and probably angry. Each partner feels that the other is overreacting, insensitive, or inconsiderate, if not abusive.

Here's an example of how shame stimulates fear. Rose could see in Carlo's sullen behavior that something happened at work. He'd been bothered by the conditions there for a while, but never wanted to talk about it when she asked. This time, she waited until he was relaxed with a drink, after a nice dinner. At last, he opened up to her.

"It's getting really bad there. I don't know if I can take the insults anymore. It's endless crap from the boss, and that asshole, Charlie. Why do I keep putting up with it? The damn job's just not worth it." He wanted to say more, but he noticed his wife's nervous expression.

"But if you quit your job, how will we pay the mortgage? We can't do it on my pay alone."

Rose proceeded to give him advice on how to handle the boss and his coworkers in a "mature way." They argued for a while, until Carlo ended it with, "I shouldn't have brought it up. Let's just watch the damn movie."

As with all intimate relationship dynamics, what was being said was not the problem. Carlo's core vulnerability—dread of failure—automatically stimulated Rose's fear of deprivation and isolation, which made him feel more like a failure. Instead of cooperating with his wife to deactivate the fear-shame dynamic, he tried to avoid his shame by shutting her out, which, of course, raised her anxiety. Rose tried to avoid her anxiety by telling him how "mature people" would react, which, of course, increased his shame.

Misunderstanding Is Unavoidable in the Toddler Brain

We're almost certain to misunderstand each other when the fear-shame dynamic locks us in the Toddler brain. For one thing, avoiding fear or shame feels very different on the inside than the way it looks on the outside. If you try to avoid feeling anxious, you'll likely come off as controlling; if you're avoiding shame, you'll appear aggressive or rejecting. For example, the higher-estrogen passenger is likely to appear nagging, criti-cal, and controlling to the higher-testosterone driver who on the outside seems insensitive, aggressive, and rejecting. In the Toddler brain, partners cannot respond to each other's deeper vulnerabilities; they're more likely to react to what they see: control, aggression, rejection.

Worse, as far as understanding each other goes, the fear-shame dynamic is obscured by the *illusion of sameness*—the assumption that events and behaviors have the same emotional meaning to both partners.

All of the above greatly influences the emotional meaning we give to events and behaviors. If you expect (or demand) that behaviors and events mean the same to your partner as they do to you, you'll be disappointed and frustrated most of the time, especially when one of you is trying to avoid fear, while the other is trying to avoid shame.

Many therapists greatly underestimate the power of the fear-shame dynamic, and some even pathologize it. Just the other day I received an email from a woman married to an angry, resentful, and, at times, emotionally abusive man. Their couples therapist, a man, explained that her fearfulness and lack of trust of her husband, who was working hard to reform, was a kind of "emotional blackmail"—a shame-driven characterization if ever I heard one. He recommended that she go into individual psychotherapy to discover the childhood origins of her fear. Similarly, female therapists are quick to label men's egos and struggles to avoid shame as developmentally immature or narcissistic and blame it on bad parenting or patriarchy. They miss the crucial point that, in the Toddler brain, partners react to each other in ways that make the situation worse; the fearful partner inadvertently makes the shame-avoidant partner feel worse, while the shame-avoidant partner inadvertently makes the fearful partner feel worse. Both lose sight of their deeper desire to be compassionate and kind to each other.

No One Self-Regulates

Self-regulation is the ability to control impulses and to calm ourselves down and cheer ourselves up. In love relationships, it requires that we hold onto self-value when we don't like our partners' behavior—and when they don't like ours—so we don't feel devalued when disappointed. It also requires that we hold onto value for our partners when we don't like their behavior—and when they don't like ours—so we don't devalue them in retaliation. We can improve interactions only with the Adult-brain stance of:

"I'm disappointed, but I'm okay, and I want us to be okay."

Unlike Toddler-brain coping mechanisms, self-regulation lets us act on the natural motivation of negative emotions. For instance, shame is a painful perception of the self as failing or inadequate; shame motivates us to learn more, try harder, or develop the skill to succeed. Most fear in intimate relationships is about isolation; fear motivates connection. These natural motivations are short-circuited by blame, denial, or avoidance, which can only produce more distance and more failure.

Without self-regulation, intimate relationship dynamics are likely to control interactions. In the worst case, we lose sight of who we are in reaction to each other: "How can I be me, while you're being you?"

Self-regulation can only occur in the Adult brain, where the sense of self is able to remain solid and cohesive while experiencing the alarm of negative emotions. Remember, the Toddler brain cannot manage the Grand Human Contradiction; all emotional issues seem like a battle between autonomy and connection. The fragile sense of self feels under siege by fear of abandonment (losing the self if rejected), fear of engulfment (losing the self if too close to others), dread of chaos (losing the self if unable to control what the partner does), and dread of submission (losing myself if I do what you want).

The dynamics of relationships provide a kind of negative self-regulation that is entirely reactive. Just as toddlers need caretakers to set limits for them, partners in Toddler-brain dynamics rely on each other to set limits. Pursuers never have to decide how much closeness they might really want; they just keep pushing and rely on distancers to determine when and where intimacy might occur. There are periods when pursuers do not feel like intimacy. Yet they cannot stop pursuing, lest the distancers run too far away. Fear of abandonment haunts the pursuer.

For their part, distancers never have to decide how much closeness they actually desire; they merely relent occasionally and give a little love, before reestablishing a "safe distance." There are times when they want more intimacy, but they're afraid to "get her/him started," as I've heard from so many clients. Fear of engulfment—losing the self in close relationships—drives the distancer.

Similarly, demanders would like to relax and stop demanding for a while, but they're afraid that if they do, everything will fall apart. Fear of chaos haunts the demander. Withdrawers would like to be more cooperative, but they're afraid to set a precedent of submitting to the demands of the demander. Dread of submission drives the withdrawer.

Thankfully, we've completed the Toddler-brain section of the book, and we're ready to move on to solution-oriented, skill-building Part II, the first chapter of which shows how to deactivate intimate relationship dynamics.

PART II
Adults in Love

CHAPTER SEVEN

Overcoming Intimate Relationship Dynamics in the Adult Brain

A s we saw in the last chapter, intimate relationship dynamics are caused by partners employing the Toddler-brain coping mechanisms of blame, denial, and avoidance. To overcome them, we must employ the Adult-brain coping mechanisms of *improve* (make the situation at least a little better), *appreciate* (something about our partners), *connect* (feel them), or *protect* them from pain and hardship. As you develop habits of coping in the Adult brain, a magical thing will happen. You'll realize that, to be happy in love, you must be compassionate and kind.

Power Love Compassion and Kindness

Evolutionary psychologists agree that *Homo sapiens* would not have survived as a species without a strong inclination to protect emotional bonds. By itself, the intelligence of early humans would have brought little success against more powerful and plentiful predators. Their primary competitors, big cats and dogs, had one or two litters a year, while our human ancestors had one child at a time, with high rates of infant mortality. In addition to being outnumbered, early humans—lacking claws, sharp teeth, speed, agility, and strength—had physical limitations that put them at a severe disadvantage. They could not see, smell, hear, jump, or climb trees as well as more powerful predators. They couldn't see at all in the dark, while big cats were nocturnal hunters. In this precarious environment, the ability to form tight-knit social units to hunt and fight collectively was crucial for survival. One person against a sabertooth tiger had no chance, but a group fighting together would prevail.

The modern emotional reflection of that primitive motivation for group-survival is *compassion.* Contemporary intimate relationships, for all their sophistication relative to early human tribal connections, can barely survive without simple compassion.

Compassion is sympathy for pain, hardship, or discomfort, with motivation to help. Beyond merely feeling sorry for loved ones, genuine compassion must support them in maintaining the balance of the Grand Human Contradiction—having an autonomous, growth-oriented, solid sense of individuality, while nurturing the relationship through compassion, kindness, and affection.

The demands on the Adult brain's capacity for compassion have increased drastically from the days when we only had to sympathize with gross pain and hardship: "Oh, a sabertooth tiger chewed off your leg, I'm so sorry."

But now we have large egos that perceive more rights and entitlements concerning personal happiness and respect from others—researchers describe it as increased narcissism. Large egos are susceptible to numerous varieties of insult, most of which are regarded as petty and insignificant in the Adult brain, however injurious they seem to the Toddler brain: "Oh, someone looked at you crooked at work, I'm so sorry."

If modern relationships can't survive without compassion, they cannot flourish without kindness.

Kindness is concern for the well-being and happiness of our partners, with motivation to help them be well and happy. Like compassion, the Adult-brain quality of kindness has undergone significant expansion just in the past generation. Sufficient for happiness in previous generations was health, stable relationships, and relative financial security. Now happiness means feeling good most of the time. Worse, many people feel entitled to have their partners *make* them feel good. With entitlement goes frustration and resentment, and the birth of the demand-withdraw dynamic.

Compassion is the lifeblood of intimate union. The high emotional reactivity of intimate relationship dynamics desensitizes partners to each other's hurt and cuts off the compassion necessary to bring life to intimate unions. Kindness provides one of the greatest joys of love: doing something kind to please your partner. When kindness gets lost in intimate relationship dynamics you hear statements like:

"I used to like sending her flowers, but now she expects it."

"I used to enjoy cooking for him, but now he thinks it's my job."

Fear of Compassion and Kindness

Many partners resent the suggestion that they should be more compassionate and kind in their relationships, although they feel quite entitled to receiving compassion and kindness.

They seem convinced that any virtue they might show would be exploited by partners hardened by the control, manipulation, rejection, and passive-aggression inherent in intimate relationship dynamics. In the Toddler brain, compassion and kindness sound a lot like becoming a doormat.

Fear of experiencing compassion and expressing kindness for a partner can be assuaged only with *self-compassion* and *self-kindness*.

Self-kindness is doing what it takes to maintain well-being, including care for your physical and emotional health. That necessarily means caring for loved ones, as we cannot be well when loved ones are not.

Self-compassion is a bit more complicated. People low in self-compassion tend to get irritated or defensive at the mere mention of compassion for others. That's because the two are really intertwined. You cannot sustain compassion for others without self-compassion, nor can you have self-compassion when cut off from your basic humane values. Without self-compassion, compassion for others can seem boundless and overwhelming. Without compassion for others, self-compassion turns to self-obsession.

Fear of becoming a doormat is greatly reduced by *compassionate assertiveness*. That's standing up for your rights and privileges in a way that appreciates and respects the rights and privileges of your partner. Here's a compassionately assertive, Adult-brain example:

"This is the restaurant I prefer, what do you think?"

Here's the Toddler-brain rendition:

"You always want to eat there. You don't care at all about what I want."

Let's take a more difficult example:

Toddler brain: "How dare you even ask if you can blow the leaves from the driveway? You know that the smell of gasoline makes me sick. How can you be so selfish and inconsiderate?"

Compassionately assertive: "I know it's a burden for you to have to rake the leaves out of the driveway, especially when you're tired. But the smell of gasoline from the leaf blower makes me nauseous. Maybe we can rake together."

Sympathetic understanding of yourself and your partner is the quickest way out of the misery of intimate relationship dynamics.

Compassion vs. Empathy

A word of caution in regard to the fear-shame dynamic: In all important matters, try to act on a higher-order compassion, rather than empathy.

Although some authors conflate the two, "empathy," as the word is typically used, is identification with the feelings of another: "I feel your pain." Necessarily limited by personal experience, empathy is more likely to obscure rather than illuminate the different vulnerabilities of each partner. Attempts to "put oneself in the shoes of the other" subjects you to the illusion of sameness and makes it more likely that you'll project your own experience onto your partner.

Emotional states are so subjective and embedded in personal experience, metabolism, genetics, physiological states, and consciousness that it can be argued, as the esteemed neuroscientist Joseph LeDoux does convincingly in *Anxious: Using the Brain to Understand and Treat Fear and Anxiety*, that we can never be sure if any two people have the same emotional experience.

Attempts at empathy are likely to yield inaccurate judgments based on your own emotional states and experience. I frequently hear something like the following from clients who consider themselves to be quite empathic when they start treatment:

"I wouldn't be afraid if that happened to me," implying that she shouldn't be, either.

"If I got fired from my job I would use it as a motivation to form stronger bonds at work the next time," implying that this is how he should see it.

Rather than trying to empathize about fear and shame, which are qualitatively different for intimate partners, we need a higher form of compassion and respect for vulnerabilities we do not share. For example, sighted people, whose brains are wired for visual imagery, cannot empathize with those born blind, whose visual cortex is wired for a different sense, and most of their other senses become keener to compensate for lack of vision. But we can feel compassion and admiration for them as they negotiate a world constructed for the sighted. And they can feel the same for us, who are relatively deficient in other senses.

With a higher level of compassion for different vulnerabilities, supporting loved ones becomes easier:

"I don't experience your fear (or dread of failure), but I care that it causes you hardship, and I'd like to help."

Without compassion, the desire to support turns into manipulation or control, and our "negotiations" retreat to the Toddler brain:

"You have to be more like me, think the way I do, feel the way I do, see the world the way I do."

Blind Spots

Mired in intimate relationship dynamics, the perspectives of both partners grow narrow and rigid. Neither will give up their negative assumptions about the other, and both remain oblivious to the way they come off to each other. You know well how our partner looks and sounds; you could write a book about it, or at least a pamphlet or blog post. But you never think, while you're in the Toddler brain, about how you look and sound when you notice that your partner is resentful, angry, anxious, or withdrawn. You don't think of how likely it is that your partner perceives you at that moment to be rejecting, condescending, manipulative, controlling, or selfish. If you are aware of your partner's perceptions at all when in the Toddler brain, blame or denial will create an impulse to argue. Indeed, a great many arguments are attempts to convince partners (if not shame or coerce them into believing) that their perceptions are wrong. Such arguments are rarely successful in changing a partner's perceptions and almost invariably lead to more resentment.

It's absolutely imperative to identify our blind spots, own them without being defensive, and adjust behavior to compensate for them. For example, a troublesome blind spot of mine is thinking about what I've written that day or looking ahead to what I'm going to say in my next workshop, while my wife is talking. I used to be defensive when she accused me of not listening, because it seemed like an unfair accusation; I could faithfully repeat everything she said. But hearing is not the same as listening. I have learned to acknowledge that mind-wandering is something I do completely without realizing it. She's important to me and I want her to feel heard. So I try to focus exclusively on her when she's talking. When my mind wanders, I appreciate when she points out my blind spot, because it reminds me to refocus and give her the attention she deserves.

Of course, your partner has blind spots, too; his or her reactions to you are also inaccurate and unfair when stuck in the Toddler brain. However tempting it may seem, reacting negatively to your partner's blind spots keeps you stuck in the toddler standoff: "No!" "Mine!"

The only way to improve our partners' blind spots is to compensate for our own with compassion and kindness.

Adjusting the Mirrors

The best strategy for reducing your blind spots is to use the reactions of your partner as an aid, like rear- and side-view mirrors.

If you believe that your partner is acting selfishly, ask yourself if you are coming off that way to your partner.

If you believe that your partner is condescending or disrespectful, ask yourself if you are being respectful and open to his or her perspective.

If you believe that your partner is devoid of compassion and caring, ask yourself if you are compassionate and caring at that moment.

If you believe that your partner is attacking, ask yourself if you're devaluing him or her, at least in your head. (Your partner can read your mind when your mind is negative. More accurately, your partner will read your body—devaluing thoughts transform emotional demeanor, which in turn changes facial expressions and body language.)

The questions above are especially important if you think your partner is acting like a jerk. If you react to a jerk like a jerk, what does that make you? If you react to Toddler-brain behavior with Toddler-brain behavior, where does that leave you?

Adjusting blind spots in emotional interactions has to be intentional, just as you intentionally adjust the rear- and side-view mirrors of your vehicle. If you drive on autopilot, on the road or in your relationships, failure to check your blind spots will lead to disaster. Putting a little care and effort into adjusting for your blind spots will get you where you want to go safely.

Bring It into the Open

Intimate relationship dynamics cannot be alleviated by discussion of "facts" or by trying to talk your partner out of his or her perceptions. And they're certainly made worse by blaming them on your partner—she's too sensitive, needy, critical, or demanding; he's too proud, sneaky, aloof, or afraid of intimacy. The best way to disarm any relationship dynamic is to recognize when it occurs, and that's just about any time you're feeling bad about the interaction. Understand that it's not your partner doing it to you. Rather, it's *happening* to both of you. Declare that your connection is important to you, cooperate to deactivate the dynamic, and reconnect.

Stand up and read the following out loud. (We tend to be more committed to declarations we make out loud while standing.)

"Hey, our dynamic got triggered. It's not you doing it to me, and it's not me doing it to you. It's happening to both of us, and together we can turn it off, because we want to connect and feel closer as we solve the problem."

Connected, you can solve the problem that may have activated the intimate relationship dynamic, because then you're on the same side. If you remain disconnected, even well-meaning and highly skilled attempts to communicate run a high risk of accidentally stimulating more fear, shame, blame, denial, pursuing, distancing, demanding, or withdrawing. If you cannot make a connection at the moment, commit to a goal of reconnecting as soon as possible.

In summary, the Adult brain is able to overcome intimate relationship dynamics by illuminating and adjusting for blind spots in our own behavior and using our partners' reactions to us as rear- and side-view mirrors. The Adult brain is able to recognize dynamics and bring them into the open, where they shrink in relation to deeper values of compassion, kindness, and connection.

Other methods of overcoming intimate relationship dynamics will be discussed in more detail in later chapters. The best way to prevent them is to balance the Grand Human Contradiction, the competing drives for autonomy and connection, and that is the subject of the next chapter.

CHAPTER EIGHT

The Adult Brain Uses Values to Balance the Grand Human Contradiction

Because the Grand Human Contradiction has strong feelings on both sides of the competing drive for autonomy and connection, we will consistently fail to balance them by trying to sort through Toddler brain feelings. Only in the Adult brain can we maintain a viable balance, by creating a set of values and sticking to them.

To grasp the psychological function of values, it's useful to think in terms of the verb *to value* rather than the noun *values*. To value someone or something goes beyond regarding that person or object as important; you also appreciate certain qualities, while investing the time, energy, effort, and sacrifice necessary for successful maintenance. If you value a da Vinci painting, you focus on its beauty and design more than the cracks in the paint, and, above all, you treat it well, making sure that it is maintained in ideal conditions of temperature and humidity, with no harsh or direct lighting. Valuing loved ones requires appreciation of their better qualities and showing care for their physical and psychological health, growth, and development.

The *experience* of value gives a heightened sense of vitality— you feel more alive looking at a beautiful sunset, connecting to a loved one, knowing genuine compassion for another person, having a spiritual experience, appreciating something creative, committing to a cause, or identifying with a community. Valuing gives a greater sense of authenticity and often a greater sense of connection. High value investment gives meaning and purpose to life, with a stronger motivation to improve, create, build, appreciate, connect, or protect.

As value investment declines, so does meaning, purpose, vitality, and motivation. You begin to function more on autopilot, with less interest and positive energy. If it declines too far, you start to feel numb or depressed. If it declines drastically, you lose the will to live. Very few people let it decline that far. Instead, we compensate for the decline in value investment by retreating to the Toddler brain, where impulse, feelings, and preferences reign supreme, and the Grand Human Contradiction goes way out of balance. For example, when I fail to appreciate and support my loved ones, I'm likely to eat or drink or work too much and blame them for my failures.

The Hierarchical Structure of Values

I believe that some values we're born with, such as the maintenance and protection of emotional bonds. (Newborns' drive to form emotional bonds supersedes the drive for food and comfort. Completely deprived of emotional bonding, they often stop eating and sometimes stop metabolizing nutrition given intravenously.) Other values we internalize in the course of life, things like friendship, loyalty, duty, a sense of community, truth, justice, and fair play. Whether learned or innate, values are hierarchical—some things are necessarily more important than others. If you don't believe that, imagine putting a carrot down the garbage disposal and then a kitten, and see if your brain doesn't make a significant distinction.

To the extent that we deviate from the hierarchical structure of values, we suffer mental discomfort, if not pain, ranging from mild irritation, impatience, resentment, anxiety, or confusion to anguish, depression, and despair. Value disturbances are factors in all these conditions, though not the only factor in most of them. For example, all depression includes value conflict and low value investment, but a number of other physiological and psychological factors also contribute to it. Yet even if the other causes ameliorate, depression—and other forms of emotional discomfort and pain—will not improve significantly without fidelity to one's deeper values.

Below are ways that we typically create value disturbances.

Acting on Feelings

Acting consistently on feelings will inevitably cause us to violate our deeper values; no one feels like acting on deeper values all the time. Feelings originate in the Toddler brain, which has no reality-testing or analytical ability to tell what's really happening or why it's happening. In the Toddler brain, we can hardly tell the difference between a distracted partner and a rejecting one, and we're likely to feel devalued by either:

"I'm not enough for you."

"You're cold, inconsiderate, and all you ever think about is yourself."

The Adult brain values the connection and is likely to behave in ways that facilitate it:

"I know you're busy, I just want you to know I'm thinking of you."

The bottom line: We have to be true to our values, even when we don't feel like it.

Choosing a Preference That Violates a Value

This usually happens when we act on feelings, but not exclusively. Sometimes we calculate the "advantages" of choosing a preference that violates a value—for instance, taking shortcuts at work that increase profits, to the unfair detriment of employees or clients. Deceit, manipulation, and other forms of dishonesty fall into this category.

Sometimes we plan to violate a deeper value under the illusion that meaning comes from preferences, rather than values. A decision to have an extramarital affair is a primary example. Excitement (of breaking a taboo) passes for meaning in the Toddler brain. Pouting or ignoring a spouse is a lesser example. The choice to pout or ignore seems to make us feel more powerful in the Toddler brain, although the violation of deeper values (caring for loved ones) ultimately disempowers. Recall an argument with your partner when you seemed to come out on top, that is, you got your way. Did you like yourself better then or when you were compassionate and kind?

Choosing a Lesser Value Over a Deeper One

As we accumulate values throughout life, they inevitably come into conflict. For example, you believe in honesty, but you don't want to hurt someone's feelings. You feel that all human beings are valuable, but you can't stand the self-righteousness of political or religious chauvinists.

No matter what the conflict, failure to maintain a hierarchy of values launches a civil war of emotions where you'll be damned if you do and damned if you don't. For example, hurting your child's feelings because her choice of music offends your aesthetic values is a violation of your deeper values, namely protecting the well-being of your child. Disagreements on one level, in this case *aesthetic*, cannot reach to a deeper level, in this case *parent-child relationship*. In other words, you won't stop loving your daughter if she likes music that you think is awful. Yet that is the implication when disputes take the following form:

"You *know* I hate that music." (Implication: All you think about is yourself. You're thoughtless and inconsiderate.)

Here the aesthetic disagreement takes on the weight of relationship betrayal (lack of caring and compassion), when the issue had nothing to do with love. A negotiation that protects the deeper value goes like this:

"You have a right to play this music and I have a right not to have to listen to it. So how can we work it out?"

This kind of negotiation with a teenager won't be problem-free, but neither will it violate your deeper values and stimulate guilt, shame, and anxiety. It has the added bonus of modeling respectful negotiation for the child.

Consider a conflict between *communal* and *intimate relationship* values. You want to go to a meeting at your civic club tonight, but your partner is sick. If you decide to go to the club, you'll feel guilty. If you stay home with your partner but do not resolve the conflict by clearly affirming what is more important, you might resent him or her for having to miss the meeting. In that unfortunate case you might come up with something like:

"If you'd worn a jacket, like I told you to do, you wouldn't have gotten sick!"

Adult-brain resolution will take the form of:

"I'm disappointed about not going to the meeting, but my partner's well-being is definitely more important to me."

Adult-brain resolution gives meaning and purpose to staying home. You might remain disappointed about missing the meeting, but you won't feel guilty, ashamed, or resentful.

A similar value conflict I see frequently in my practice ensnares parents who have to put their young children in daycare. In the Toddler brain, value conflicts almost always degenerate into autonomy-connection struggles. If parents who feel guilty about leaving their children in daycare assert their "right to self-actualize," the guilt from the connection side of the struggle will merely go underground and come out as resentment, anxiety, or depression. Rather, the conflict must be resolved in deference to the deeper value:

"I'm disappointed about having to put my child in daycare, but working enables me to provide sustenance and a better life for her."

Irrational thoughts of being a bad parent might sometimes recur, for example, when you approach the daycare center. Each time they occur, they must have an answer that makes the value —a better life for your child—more important than the uncomfortable feeling about putting her in daycare while you work.

Adults who retreat to the Toddler brain under stress are continually confused about value conflicts. For example, Jackson started treatment as the result of an altercation with his wife. Irina wanted to join a church group, which would take her out of the house one night a week. Jackson accused her of not caring about their marriage, arguing that they were not spending enough time together. To Irina it felt like Jackson was depriving her of communal and spiritual connection, though of course she did not use those words. Their Toddler-brain standoff went like this:

"If you cared about our marriage, you'd stay home."

"If I stay home, you'll just ignore me and watch TV, and I'll be missing out on something that's important to me."

In Toddler-brain standoffs, nobody can "win" or feel valued. Irina would resent not joining the church group if she gave in, and Jackson would resent her if she joined the group.

On the deeper value level, it's easier to see that the real problem was not the amount of time they spent together but the quality of their connection. If they felt more connected, Jackson would not have minded his wife's joining the church group, because he would have supported her desire for spiritual and communal growth. The solution to the problem was forging a closer connection.

In the Toddler brain, Jackson thought he could get his wife to feel more connected by devaluing her and making it less pleasant to be with him. (A sure way to tell that you're turning a value conflict into an autonomy-connection struggle is needing adrenaline, anger, or alcohol to assert your perceived right.) We worked in therapy to help him be more compassionate, loving, and kind. This increased his self-value, while making him feel more autonomous, which, in turn, makes him more attractive. At the same time, his loving behavior strengthened their connection. It was then easy for him to support Irina's desire to join the church group. His supportive attitude made the time they spent together more valuable to both of them.

Why Deeper Values Matter the Most

Deeper values contribute enormously to who we are. When true to them, we have a solid sense of self. What we typically mean by "you're not yourself" is behavior or attitudes that violate a person's values. Values help us feel authentic and valuable when we uphold them, but they stab us with guilt, shame, and anxiety when we ignore or violate them, as we're bound to do in the Toddler brain.

This is really a brilliant system to ensure the survival of the most social of all species: You feel good when you do good (think and act in accordance with your deepest values) and feel bad when you don't. It's a psychosocial system that would produce peace and harmony in the world, if only we hadn't developed the means to confound it.

Alas, we've learned countless ways to feel good, however temporarily, without doing good. For example, alcohol, drugs, and sexual affairs make us feel good for a little while. We have nearly endless ways to avoid feeling bad when we violate our deeper values. Bad feelings are temporarily relieved by adrenaline arousal (anger or resentment), drugs, obsession, compulsive behavior, and of course, blame, denial, and avoidance.

No matter how much we blame, deny, and avoid, our strongest emotions are guardians of our deeper values. We feel better when we're protective, compassionate, and kind to loved ones and worse when we're not.

The Deepest Value: The Most Important Thing About You

To establish the hierarchy of your personal values, ask your-self the following two questions:

CRUCIAL QUESTION #1:

What is the *most* important thing about me as a person?

- Is it a personal quality, like honesty, integrity, industry, friendliness, ambition?

- Is it a personal talent or gift, like intelligence, skills, intuition, savvy, street smarts, athleticism?

- Is it work accomplishments or successes?

- Is it compassion, kindness, and love for the significant people in your life?

If you did not choose the last option, would you rather your loved ones admire you for the first three options but doubt that you love and care about them? Or would you prefer that they recognize that you have flaws and are capable of making mistakes and suffering failures, like all humans, yet—despite your human shortcomings—they always know that you care about them and want what is best for them?

CRUCIAL QUESTION #2:

What is the *most* important thing about my life?

If you have trouble with this question, choose what you would want your eulogy to mention or what you would like inscribed on your tombstone:

- What you gave to the world or what you took from it

- What you improved or what you made worse

- Who you criticized or what you appreciated

- What you created or what you destroyed

Answering these crucial questions should tease out your deepest values—the most important things to and about you. Fidelity to your deepest values is the key to balancing the opposing drives for autonomy and connection. We feel autonomous when honoring our deepest values, and that naturally leads to fair, compassionate, and kind behavior, which strengthens connections to significant others.

Other Important Things

If you can answer the above questions with conviction, purpose, and passion, and if your behavior is consistent with your answers, then your life, no doubt, feels completely genuine. You are one of the fortunate who continually grow, learn, produce, create, and care. You very rarely question your own value or anyone else's. You routinely regulate negative emotions by investing interest and effort in people and things that are important to you and thereby create value in the world around you. You acknowledge alarms and signals from the Toddler brain but always test their reality and fidelity to your values in the Adult brain.

Those of us less fortunate have to think long and hard to answer the crucial questions and often become appalled at how little our behavior reflects what we most deeply believe to be important. The negative emotions that we blame on stress, bad days, excess weight, society, coworkers, neighbors, and family come largely from ignoring or violating what is most important to and about us.

Here's an example. When the most important thing about driving is to get to a destination as quickly as possible, people tend to drive aggressively. They devalue their emotional well-being by increasing the stress of driving. They devalue their safety and that of every person—every *child*—in every car they pass. They ignore both the general warning of their emotional discomfort (to value *more*) and the specific message—develop solutions to any problems that being late might cause. In the Toddler brain, they'll blame their discomfort on other drivers, the design of the highway, their bosses, their spouses, getting up late, or their "own stupidity." Their emotions can no longer guide their behavior to conform to what is most important to and about them. Instead, they seem to be instruments of punishment, unfairly controlled by situations or other people.

The Toddler brain invariably confuses the nuanced challenges of life with assaults on autonomy. The result is a sense of powerlessness that impairs thinking, performance, and concentration. Adults in the Toddler brain work less efficiently, become exhausted more easily, and are less than sweet to their kids when they get home. Interestingly, traffic studies show that aggressive drivers arrive at their destinations only seconds before safe drivers. How many times have you stopped at a red light just behind a driver who had cut you off or whizzed by you?

In the Adult brain, the most important thing about driving is attending to the safety of everyone on the road.

Don't Confuse Values with Goals and Intentions

Many people get stuck in the Toddler brain by confusing its alarms with their conscious goals and intentions. For instance, Sal came to my office about a "communication problem" with his wife, Marie. He described a terrible altercation that began with what he characterized as his "harsh but *right*" reproach:

"This is the third time I've asked you to look at the account balance before you write a check! We're overdrawn again!"

His *goal* in this interaction was to get Marie to take more care with the checkbook. His *intention* was to let her know that he was upset because she hadn't. But in his Toddler brain the problem became one of autonomy rather than negotiating with someone he loved; he felt personally devalued by her behavior. In retaliation, he tried to make her feel bad about herself for making the mistake. Marie's response, of course, was defensive. After some mutual name-calling, she promised to be more careful, but she felt humiliated, like she was submitting to his anger.

Toddler-brain power struggles almost always produce passive-aggressive behavior on the part of the one who has to submit. Marie's "forgetting" was not on purpose. On many occasions in the past, the loud alarm of the Toddler brain made Sal interpret the normal distractedness of a busy working mother as a personal affront to him, prompting his attack mode. After only a couple of repetitions of this dance, Marie associated the checkbook with humiliation. The Toddler brain will do almost anything to *avoid* thinking about humiliation. Marie automatically sought less shame-invoking things to occupy her mind, which made her more likely to forget about the checking account balance. The more often she forgot, the more he attacked, and the more he fooled himself with the "rightness" of his goals and intentions. He made it worse by choosing his words according to one of the thousands of bulleted lists of "communication skills" published on the Internet, which added an extra layer of self-righteousness to his "I-statement" attacks.

"I feel you never listen to me. I feel disrespected."

Sal's problem with his wife was about values, not "communication." In his Adult brain, the most important thing about this interaction would have been to model cooperation and respect. Attack motivations can evoke submission and fear, along with resentment and an impulse to retaliate, but never cooperation and respect.

In addition to their value disturbances, Jackson and Sal in the examples above inadvertently trapped themselves in the Toddler brain with the metaphors they used to organize their beliefs. How to use metaphors to achieve a Power love is the topic of the brief chapter that follows.

CHAPTER NINE

The Adult Brain Uses Metaphors to Balance the Grand Human Contradiction

The Adult brain loves metaphors, where a word or phrase means something other than what it literally denotes. In addition to stimulating higher levels of mental processing, metaphors elevate discourse beyond mere relating of facts. They afford us a richer expression of concepts, perceptions, and emotions. Used well, they deepen communication, advance knowledge, and inspire us. To paraphrase Tennessee Williams, metaphor is the natural language of the arts. Without metaphors, the written word would have the vitality of technical journals. Conversations would be banal or vulgar or hopelessly complex and boring.

Even in their most rudimentary form, metaphors are completely unfathomable to the Toddler brain. If a young child overhears something like, "Life is hard," he/she might think of a stick or the wood floor or the refrigerator door but won't grasp how any of these relate to life or even what the word "life" means. Unfortunately, adults in the Toddler brain apply the same sort of literalness to metaphors. Instead of deepening appraisals of reality, metaphors degrade them. During my many years of clinical practice, I've made a habit of asking people at intake what metaphors described their lives. Typical responses have been:

"Life is a minefield."

"Life is a journey."

"Life is a three-ring circus."

"Life is a race."

"Life is a marathon."

"Life is a battle."

The Adult brain understands metaphors like these well enough. But the Toddler brain sounds alarms about danger-ous minefields and battles, the uncertainties of journeys, the chaos of a three-ring circus, the gruel of the race, the exhaus-tion of the marathon, and so forth. The alarms are typically subtle, experienced more like a general unease or tension, but they nevertheless distort appraisals of reality and make us ever ready to blame, deny, and avoid.

Metaphors that activate the old autonomy-connection struggle sound the most intrusive Toddler-brain alarms:

"Love melds us into one."

"Only the strong survive."

Because metaphors are critical to understanding the world around us, choosing the wrong ones can make the autonomy-connection struggle seem like standing astride two galloping horses.

The "wrong metaphors" are those that reinforce Toddler-brain behaviors. An example I'm sure you've heard of is the description of angry outbursts as "letting off steam." This unfortunate metaphor derives from a nineteenth-century understanding of emotions, when the dominant technology was the steam engine. The theory held that, without frequent "release," emotions "build up" to dangerous levels until they cause an explosion, like a stream engine with a stuck valve. The steam engine metaphor led to widely discredited "therapeutic" techniques like punching pillows, dolls, or dummies and using foam baseball bats to club imaginary adversaries. Many studies have shown that such techniques actually make people feel angrier and more hostile, not to mention more entitled to act out their anger. Rather than "getting it out of your system," repetition forms habits that make Toddler-brain processing more dominant and automatic.

Scientific evidence shows that emotions are not like steam engines at all. Rather, they function more like muscles—the more you use them, the stronger the neural connections underlying them grows. The more you focus on any emotion, the more likely it becomes that you'll frequently re-experience it by habit.

The best way to mitigate Toddler-brain influence on appraisals of reality—and subsequent choices of behavior—is to base metaphors on values, rather than transitory feelings. The following should clarify the difference between value-based and feelings-based metaphors. These are the implicit feelings-based metaphors that intensified and prolonged the painful standoffs between Sal and his wife:

"A good husband is like a rock," which made him hard and intransigent.

"If a husband seems weak, he'll be manipulated," which made him insensitive to the internal world of his wife.

"Marriage is like a movie thriller; you have to drive hard to avoid a bad end," which made him too forceful.

We replaced these dysfunctional metaphors with those based on his deeper values:

"A good husband is like a champion, a nurse, a guide, and a shade tree."

"Marriage is like a handful of seeds. With nurturing and care, they develop into a lovely garden."

"Marriage is a movie with some comedy, mystery, excitement, sorrow, pain, love, and beauty."

The Toddler-brain metaphor that had made it tough for Jackson (also described above) was:

"Love is a meal we must eat together," which made him feel hungry and needy.

The Adult-brain metaphor we developed was:

"Love is a lifeline that keeps us connected, even when we're apart."

Using Metaphors that Balance the Grand Human Contradiction

When values fuel metaphors, we use the power of the Adult brain to improve and enrich our experience. Here are a couple of examples that help balance the drives for autonomy and connection.

Life is like a flower garden; if you nurture it, it sweetens your time on earth. You don't *need* the flowers to sustain life; you *desire* them to enrich your experience. Autonomy is strengthened by choosing to nurture the orchard, which, in turn, brings connection to those family members who also choose to nurture the orchard. Some of what you do will be for other people, but most of what you do will be to nurture the orchard that enhances your experience of being alive.

Love is like a musical duet. In a duet, both musicians are able to make beautiful music on their own. But together they make something greater than either can do alone: *harmony.*

Harmony is an appealing combination of elements in a whole. In music, it's an arrangement of sounds pleasing to the ear. Harmony in intimate relationships is more about emotional tone and atmosphere than expressions of love or specific behaviors. It's about both partners thriving and growing into the best musicians they can be. You stop making harmony when the Toddler brain dominates the relationship, simply because it cannot balance the drives for autonomy and connection. In the Toddler brain, all you can do is try to criticize or stonewall the violin into becoming the cello, and vice versa.

Harmony rises from partners attuned to their deepest values, which will necessarily include compassion and kindness for each other. The foundation of relationship harmony is frequent notes of compassion and kindness, focused on the long-term best interests of both partners. Focusing on compassion and kindness, rather than on being right or wrong, creates the sort of relationship harmony that keeps the drives for autonomy and connection in balance, and creates *Power love.*

CHAPTER TEN

Closeness and Distance:
The Laws of Emotional Bonds

Most of the time we're not aware of the small emotions we experience whenever in proximity to loved ones. Routine emotional responses to our partners are mostly low grade and outside awareness, yet they're ever present, drawing us together or pulling us apart.

Though hard to discern even when we stop to reflect on them, small emotional responses do more to create the "atmosphere" or "climate" of the relationship than the feelings we know we're having. The cold shoulders between arguments often do more damage than the arguments themselves. Researchers cite the "climate" of a relationship as one of the most important factors in marital satisfaction and dissatisfaction. For instance, an argument about how to spend money can be destructive if the climate of the relationship is hostile. The parties are likely to engage in devaluing comments and fail to resolve anything without a great deal of resentment on both sides:

"You can be so stupid about money."

"You can be so selfish and unreasonable."

Once again, altering the language in the above examples without changing the emotional climate of the relationship would likely make the partners feel manipulated.

When the climate of the relationship is positive, the same discussion can be beneficial, leading to the exchange of ideas and remedial action:

"I'm not sure what the problem is in spending money on something we don't need but would enjoy. Can you help me understand?"

"I don't think we can afford it."

"Then let's look at what we're spending and see if we can cut back on something else."

In the context of a sanguine relationship climate, this couple did valuable joint budgeting by working together, which every couple with money issues should strive to do.

Emotional Climate Causes Closeness or Distance

The emotions we're likely to be aware of when in proximity to an intimate partner serve as *distance regulators*—signals of closeness and distance. In *Power love*, partners act consistently on the signals that bring them closer rather than those that create distance.

The primary distance regulators of intimate relationships are low-grade guilt and shame, which usually manifest as feelings of irritation or impatience. By the time we're adults, an experience of subtle guilt and shame has generalized beyond original causes to be stimulated by any number of environmental cues (a door closing, a distracted partner, a whiny child) or by transient thoughts and memories. In the Toddler brain, we won't notice guilt and shame getting worse, because the toddler coping mechanisms get triggered so quickly. Remember, the primary function of coping mechanisms is to mitigate painful feelings. We'll *avoid* (through work, alcohol, over-involvement with children or friends), or *deny*: "I'm okay; you'll get over it." But most likely, we'll *blame* each other for not "meeting my needs." In any case, the intensity of negative emotions is fueled by the underlying guilt and shame.

To appreciate the distance-regulating function of subtle guilt and shame, try this experiment. (You probably won't be aware of the deeper guilt or shame, but you should notice the irritation or impatience on the surface.) Get closer—by showing interest, appreciation, affection, or protection—and guilt and shame should disappear, that is, you won't feel as irritated or impatient. If you dare to create more distance (distraction, criticism, resentment, or jealousy), which I don't recommend, the guilt and shame, expressed as resentment, anger, or contempt, will get worse.

Guilt and shame are unavoidable in love relationships because they drive what I call the Laws of Emotional Bonds. Okay, they're not really laws, but they are compelling internal processes that have less to do with individual psychology than survival of the species; the capacity for guilt and shame developed in our brains at a time when losing emotional bonds meant certain death by starvation or sabertooth tiger. That's why when we get dumped in a relationship, especially prior to full prefrontal cortex development, part of us feels like we're going to die. (Tragically, romantic breakup is the cause of many teenage suicides and murder-suicides in young adulthood.) The same survival associations of species history are recapitulated for each individual in the helplessness of toddlerhood. Perceived damage to emotional bonds is overwhelming to the Toddler brain and certain to thrust children into temper tantrums. Guilt and shame over loss of emotional bonds feels like life or death.

> **LAW #1** | *Whenever we threaten emotional bonds we experience some level of guilt.*

A few of the ways we threaten emotional bonds is by losing interest in loved ones, failing at compassion, breaching trust, failing to trust, diminishing love, avoiding intimacy, or failing to protect loved ones. Guilt from any of these is automatic, although we obscure it with blame, denial, and avoidance. Remember, guilt evolved in the human brain as part of the glue that holds emotional bonds together, keeping us in families, clans, and tribes, which increased chances of survival.

> **LAW #2** | *Whenever we sense that a loved one threatens emotional bonds, we experience shame.*

Shame occurs when emotional bonds are strained or severed. When a loved one ignores, rejects, devalues, harms, loses interest, withholds compassion, fails to trust, breaches trust, avoids intimacy, fails to protect, or doesn't seem to care, we experience some level of the shame of rejection, although, once again, Toddler-brain blame, denial, and avoidance are likely to conceal it.

Displays of shame no doubt evolved to reinstate emotional bonds and keep the clan together for the greater good (in terms of strength and cooperation). The toddler who covers her face and cries in shame prompts affection and comfort from caregivers.

In intimate relationships, displays of shame, usually in the form of remorse, are key to successful apologies for all but the most minor offenses. If the offended partner knows that you feel bad, it seems safer to trust again. Many people automatically begin a sincere apology with:

"I feel so bad. . . ."

One recent study showed that a majority of women found two facial expressions attractive in photographs of men: success and shame. The latter surprised a lot of researchers who misunderstand the role of shame in love. Shame tells a potential partner that you care about emotional bonds and will make a bid to reinforce them when they are threatened. Of course, a look of success implies that the bonds won't be threatened very often. In fact, shame and success are opposite sides of the same coin in love relationships. (Who could love a shameless partner?) Successful partners have learned to use shame as motivation to succeed in love, that is, they've learned to replace the discomfort of shame with the comfort of connection.

In the same study, men found happy facial expressions to be the most attractive feature of prospective partners. The happy expression makes them feel successful as protectors.

Psychologically, shame is a reorganizing signal, a warning that our thoughts or actions are failing to maintain social bonds. It tells us to do or think something else. In love relationships, it tells us to do something that will strengthen emotional connection, that is, be more compassionate, kind, loving, supportive, and so on.

But in Toddler-brain relationships, we perceive guilt and shame as punishments for assertions of autonomy, rather than motivations to strengthen the emotional bond. As long as the Toddler brain is in control, the urges to blame, deny, or avoid will not be seen for what they are: attempts to reduce guilt or shame. Instead, the very impulse to blame, deny, or avoid seems to "prove" that our partners are wrong, unfair, or untrustworthy. If I feel like blaming you, you *must* be bad, so I will consider only evidence that "proves" your culpability and disregard anything to the contrary.

You're probably aware of your partner trying to reduce his or her guilt and shame by blaming you but less aware of doing the same yourself.

It's *Not* About Right or Wrong

In regard to the function of attachment emotions—to preserve emotional bonds that were once necessary for survival—it doesn't matter who is right or wrong, fair or unfair, trustworthy or unfit for trust. Whenever we threaten emotional bonds or perceive a threat to them, no matter what the reason, we experience guilt and/or shame. But wait, it gets worse. Guilt and shame induce states of vulnerability, which make the brain hypersensitive to possible threats. (The more vulnerable we feel, the more threat we're likely to perceive.) The threatened ego shifts into defensive resentment or anger, fueled by guilt or shame, within milliseconds, which is far too fast for conscious awareness. We may know we're resentful (usually not) or angry (usually) but are unlikely to fathom that we also feel guilty and ashamed. The most reliable indicator of low-grade guilt or shame is resentment or anger. Resentment and anger are the flames, guilt and shame are the fuel.

Guilt and shame are stimulated automatically by perceived threats to the emotional bond, so don't mislead yourself by thinking that you've got no reason to feel guilt or shame. You may not have a "reason," but the function of shame in intimate relationships has nothing to do with rationality and everything to do with survival of the bond. If you ignore, devalue, deceive, harm, or simply fail to care for your intimate partner, there is guilt beneath your resentment, anger, anxiety, or depression. Add shame to the mix if you perceive that your partner did any of the above, either proactively or in reaction to your behavior.

Guilt and shame cannot function as motivations to connect when obscured by blame, denial, or avoidance. Instead, they become fuel for the eternal flame of resentment.

Disarming the Jealousy Complex

Another common distance regulator in love relationships is simple jealousy. In Chapter Five, I distinguished between two kinds of jealousy. The simple variety emerges in early toddlerhood and occurs in all love relationships to some extent, serving as a reliable signal of distance in the relationship. Absent chronic resentment, it motivates partners to reconnect. Complex jealousy, on the other hand, motivates control and coercion, which profoundly block emotional connection.

Because complex jealousy wreaks harm on the self and the relationship, it takes dedicated effort to defang it. (As we saw in Chapter Five, the fangs grow larger when you indulge in jealousy, especially when you justify it.) The following is a difficult but effective formula for freeing yourself from the emotional maelstrom, which, unchecked, will ruin your relationship and possibly make you crazy in the process.

Distrust obsessions. They greatly distort reality. If you can't stop thinking about your partner flirting with someone else, at least distrust the thought processes. Try to step back and observe yourself obsessing. Write the obsessive thoughts down in longhand—slowing the rapid flow of obsessions makes them more amenable to reality testing. After you write them down, read them aloud into a digital recorder. When you play it back, the sound of your voice uttering the obsessions will likely invoke the Adult brain, where you have greater reality testing and regulatory power. Give each sentence in the obsession an Adult-brain answer.

"She's with some guy right now." Emphasize the answer: "She's more likely at work."

"He's angry when I come into the room because he's looking at porn." Answer: "He gets irritable if he's abruptly interrupted, because it's hard for him to refocus. I'll gently call to him before I enter the next time and see if he's still angry."

Prevent obsessions by regulating core hurts. Complex jealousy floats on a sea of what I call "core hurts"—feeling *unlovable* and *inadequate* (as an intimate partner). Everyone has core hurts, except perhaps sociopaths who are incapable of prosocial emotions like love, compassion, guilt, and shame.

The great mistake of pop psychology is its preoccupation with how we might have acquired core hurts. You'll find thousands of books and articles speculating that core hurts come from bad parenting, mean siblings, abuse, bullying, or bad relationships. Any such explanation might make you feel temporarily validated, but you might end up feeling like a powerless victim with a lifetime sentence of resentment. Whether any of these so-called explanations are valid causal factors is beside the point. They ignore the primary function of guilt and shame in love relationships, which is to motivate loving behavior. Regardless of what happened to you in the past, there is simply no way to feel genuinely worthy of love or adequate as an intimate partner without doing what makes you worthy of love, namely behaving in ways that are compassionate, kind, and loving.

Attempts to cope with core hurts in the Toddler brain guarantee that jealousy will balloon to outrageous proportions. If, in my heart, I don't believe that I'm worthy of love, how can I believe someone who says she loves me? I'll assume that she doesn't know the real me, or she wants something else (my money, house, car, or socks), or she wants some*one* else.

Because I cannot possibly be enough for her, I'll think that she must be seeking fulfillment somewhere else. I'll continually hunt for clues of her "deceit," because no one could love the real me. And of course I'll be less compassionate, kind, and loving and, as a result, feel inadequate.

When you're attacked by the painful feeling of unworthiness, *before* it stimulates a cycle of jealous obsessions and fantasies of revenge, ask yourself, *out loud*:

"What can I do to feel more lovable and adequate (as an intimate partner)?"

Just uttering the words will make it clear that devaluing, belittling, hassling, or punishing your loved one is unlikely to make you feel like a lovable and adequate partner.

To feel worthy of love—and adequate as an intimate partner—begin by trying as hard as you can to see the world through your partner's eyes. Appreciate that he or she probably feels unlovable and inadequate at the same time you do, if for no other reason than living with a jealous partner.

Once you have a realistic sense of your partner's perspective, make a list of times in the past when you felt lovable and identify your behavior that went with the feeling. Whatever you were doing when you felt lovable can be described as *improving, appreciating, connecting,* or *protecting*. You must do one of these—improve, appreciate, connect, or protect—when you experience jealousy.

Focus on compassion, not trust. If you suffer from complex jealousy, you no longer have the confidence to trust. All attempts to trust will be doomed to failure, until you've developed Adult-brain habits of loving. Focus on compassion for yourself and your loved one. After a long period of self-compassion and compassion for your partner, trust will sneak up on you. You'll wake up one day and realize that you're once again a trusting person, provided you behave consistently in ways that make you feel worthy of love.

Follow the self-correcting motivation of simple jealousy to reconnect. Be more compassionate, supportive, cooperative, and loving. Be mindful of what you love about your partner. Be the partner you most want to be.

Like anything repeated over time, the obsessional element of complex jealousy has the effect of training the brain to think jealous thoughts. To overcome complex jealousy, we must literally retrain the brain. The following technique can help.

Overcoming Complex Jealousy

Record answers to your jealous thoughts with Adult-brain answers. (Examples: "She's with some guy right now" is answered by: *"She's more likely at work."* "He's angry when I come into the room because he's looking at porn" is answered by: *"He gets irritable if he's abruptly interrupted because it's hard for him to refocus. I'll gently call to him before I enter the next time and see if he's still angry."*)

Jealous thought	Answer

Threats of feeling unlovable and inadequate underlie complex jealousy. It's imperative to use jealous feelings as a motivation to do whatever makes you feel lovable.

List behaviors that make you feel lovable (examples: acts of caring, nurturing, support, encouragement, compassion, kindness).

1. _____

2. _____

3. _____

4. _____

5. _____

Overcoming Jealousy Log

Jealous feeling	What I did to feel lovable
1.	
2.	
3.	
4.	
5.	

Jealous feeling	How I connected with my partner
1.	
2.	
3.	
4.	
5.	

Once you've established your lists, practice the associations using the **TIP** technique for building new habits, as described in Chapter Thirteen (see page 147).

Resentment and the Laws of Emotional Bonds

Resentment in general stems from a perception of unfairness— you're not getting something good you deserve, or you're getting something bad you don't deserve, or you perceive an unequal distribution of resources, praise, reward, or privilege. Of course, it's a bit more complicated in love relationships. Most resentment in love arises from the guilt and shame of violating the Laws of Emotional Bonds. If you're willing to go by self-report, what couples in committed relationships resent the most are things like unilateral decision making, management of resources (who spends how much on what, when, and where), division of labor and responsibility (work within and outside the home), sex, parenting, and in-laws. These things can certainly stimulate resentment, but they do not cause it.

The ultimate cause of resentment in love relationships is loss of the way we felt when falling in love. I don't mean the rapture of Toddler-brain infatuation, which, though intense and often pleasant, is too unstable to endure. What we lose as resentment builds in love relationships is a cornerstone of the sense of self: *feeling worthy of love*. In the beginning, love relationships make us feel lovable. Regardless of our faults and foibles, we feel worthy of the love we receive. What we don't realize is this:

It isn't being loved that makes us feel lovable; it's *loving*.

It's a hard distinction to see most of the time. Being loved makes it so much easier to be loving that we can easily miss which provides the greater boost to self-value. Unless you feel lovable, feeling loved will not feel good, beyond a shallow ego stroke. It won't feel good because it inevitably stirs *guilt* for getting something you don't really feel you deserve and, worse, the *shame* of inadequacy, because you don't feel able to return the love you get. The wellspring of resentment in love relationships is blaming this guilt and shame on our partners.

The great paradox of resentment in love relationships is that we feel entitled to something we don't feel worthy of—not while we're resentful. The more resentful we get, the more entitled and less worthy we feel.

If you're resentful in a love relationship, you're not getting much compassion, kindness, caring, support, or affection. It's also a pretty good bet that you're not giving very much of those things, at least not while you're resentful. All you can do to improve the former is to invest more in the latter. That won't always work to improve your relationship as much as you would like, but anything else will damage it further.

The key questions to ask in evaluating your love relationship are:

Am I being the person and partner I most want to be?

Am I giving as much compassion, kindness, caring, and affection as I'm getting?

Compare these questions to the Toddler-brain cant:

"I'm not getting my needs met."

Which mindset is more likely to improve your relationship?

It's Compassion or Resentment

Most committed relationships end in a whimper, not a bang. The final rupture is not caused by too much anger or abuse or infidelity. Rather, most die a slow, agonizing death from too little compassion.

Compassion is simple appreciation of the basic human frailty we all share, which is why giving it makes you feel more humane and less isolated. Love relationships cannot even form—beyond superficial attraction—without compassion. Think of when you were dating someone you eventually came to love. Suppose you had to call that person and report that your parents had died. If your date responded with, "Well, that's tough, call me when you get over it," would you have fallen in love with that person? Chances are, you fell in love with someone who seemed to care about how you felt, especially when you felt bad.

Most of what you fight about now is not really money or sex or in-laws or raising the kids. Those are common problems that seem insurmountable only when you're hurt. What causes the hurt, that is, what you really fight about, is the impression that your partner doesn't care how you feel. When someone you love is not compassionate, it feels like betrayal.

As compassion decreases, resentment rises automatically. As compassion rises, resentment automatically decreases, and problems become negotiable. If unfettered by the better angels of our nature, resentment inevitably turns into contempt.

Contempt, as we saw in Chapter Four, is disdain for the hurt of others, due to judgments about their "lower moral standing," "character defects," "mental instability," "ignorance," or general "unworthiness." Contempt is powered by a low-grade but consistent drip of adrenaline. So long as the adrenaline lasts, you feel more confident and self-righteous in blaming your bad feelings on your partner. But you also feel less humane. And when the adrenaline wears off, you feel depressed.

By the time couples come to our boot camps for chronic resentment, anger, or emotional abuse, they have developed entrenched habits of protecting their respective vulnerabilities by devaluing each other. They try to justify their contempt with "evidence" that the partner is selfish, lazy, narcissistic, crazy, abusive, and so on. Mutual resentment makes them both feel chronically criticized and attacked, although neither really wants to attack the other. They rationalize their bad behavior as mere reactions to the awful behavior of the other. Their defenses so automatically justify their resentment and contempt that they cannot see each other's hurt. Neither can they see that their resentment and contempt have cut them off from their deeper values and made them into someone they are not.

The only way out, whether the couple stays in the relationship or not, is to focus on compassion—not to manipulate change in the other—but to feel more humane and to reconnect with their deepest values. If they are able to use the skills learned in the boot camps to do that, they can change the climate of the relationship and effectively use the relationship skills highlighted in the rest of this book.

CHAPTER ELEVEN

Binocular Vision

*B*inocular vision is the ability to hold our partners' perspectives alongside our own and to see ourselves through our partners' eyes.

How important is binocular vision to love relationships? Just compare it to monocular vision. Looking through one eye reduces the area you can see. It also distorts depth perception among the objects you see and dampens your ability to see movement. It's harder to notice these effects just by covering up one eye, because your brain fills in the missing information with guesses of what the other eye would see. The differences are more obvious when comparing a telescope to a pair of binoculars.

Telescopes magnify everything in the monocular cone of vision, thereby distorting depth perception. Because you have to move the telescope with the moving object, it's difficult to assess speed and direction of movement. By contrast, binoculars present dual perceptions to the visual cortex, which it then reverses and converts into fairly accurate depth perception—you can tell how far away objects really are. The movement of objects across a wide field of perception lends more accuracy to assessments of speed and direction.

Binocular vision in relationships makes you smarter. In the wild, it's mostly predatory animals, like big cats and wolves, that developed binocular vision—eyes in the front of their heads. This great advantage equips them for detecting movement and judging distances, which helps them stalk, chase, anticipate speed and direction of prey, and pounce. Predatory animals are smarter than their prey, largely because their brains grew by processing more information, which then enabled them to have a high-protein diet for still more neuronal growth and more intelligence.

Binocular vision in relationships calms anxiety, builds confidence, and provides depth and dynamism. Prey animals who have one eye on either side of their heads suffer a distinct disadvantage in vision, which they make up for with the size of their herds—what they lack in acuity they make up for in quantity. Besides the obvious fact that they can be killed by predators, part of the reason that prey animals are more nervous and skittish (even when born free of predators in captivity) is that they cannot trust their vision to give them enough information to know when they are safe. Monocular vision enhances anxiety. In human relationships, monocular perspectives breed nervousness, suspicion, complex jealousy, and eventual paranoia, which can make you think that your partner is out to make your life miserable.

Only binocular vision can give an accurate picture of your relationship. Only binocular vision allows you to see more deeply into the heart of your partner, while observing your part in the interactive cycle.

My clients often resist binocular vision at first, out of fear that they will lose something if they truly understand their partners' perspectives. With binocular vision, you never give up your perspective or lose sight of it; you *add* to it, through a deeper understanding of your partner's.

Chances are, if you're reading this book, you've become stuck in monocular vision. But you're certainly not trapped in it. You can change the way your brain is wired and begin to see life through a more enriching lens that includes your partner's experience as well as your own. I've seen it happen thousands of times.

Start by appreciating the fact that you have a potent *internal sensor* of your partner's perspective. The emotional bond that keeps you together acts as a conduit of emotion contagion and reciprocity. When your partner feels something, you will automatically feel something very similar. If it's negative, your habituated response will likely come from the Toddler brain. Instead of reacting to your partner, use the gift of your internal sensor to activate the Adult brain. Here are examples:

"I'm frustrated, which means you probably feel frustrated, too."

"I feel rejected, which means you probably feel overwhelmed or distracted."

"I feel controlled, which means you feel anxious or out of control."

In the Toddler brain, we blame our vulnerable emotions on our partners:

"You make me so angry or resentful."

In binocular vision, we *own our anxiety, fear, and shame* and *understand what they stimulate in our partners*:

"I'm so sensitive that things sometimes send my anxiety through the roof. I know you're uncomfortable too, but I'm sure we can come up with something we can both feel okay about." (Let me repeat the caveat: Don't worry about the specific words you use. Rather, focus on your motivation to connect and cooperate. If you sincerely want to connect and cooperate, your word choice will matter little.)

Steven Stosny

Owning vulnerability and acknowledging your partner's discomfort gives him or her a chance to be compassionate, rather than defensive.

Binocular Vision Provides Relationship Depth

Relationship depth is that which lies beneath the surface of interactions, including the vulnerability that stimulates the toddler coping mechanisms of blame, denial, and avoidance.

Because binocular vision activates the Adult brain, it regulates the impulse to blame, deny, and avoid when deeper vulnerabilities are stimulated. In other words, we're able to see beneath the surface of superficial Toddler-brain reactions.

Monocular vision: I feel frustrated. My partner doesn't get it or doesn't care or is too selfish or too stupid or too crazy.

Binocular vision: I feel frustrated, which means my partner feels frustrated, too. (It's rarely the case where only one of you feels frustrated.)

Monocular vision: I feel rejected. My partner doesn't love me or is insensitive, selfish, or abusive.

Binocular vision: I feel rejected, which means my partner probably feels overwhelmed, distracted, or rejected.

Monocular vision: I feel controlled. My partner is a control freak, obsessive-compulsive, abusive, a psychopath.

Binocular vision: I feel controlled, which means my partner feels anxious or feels out of control.

Never trust your own perspective if you cannot see your partner's alongside it. Even if completely correct, your perspective is incomplete, lacking depth and dynamism. The only complete reality of your relationship is both perspectives together.

Some of my clients are hesitant about binocular vision at first, out of fear that they will lose something if they truly understand their partners' perspectives. They sometimes confuse binocular vision with simple perspective-taking. The research of John Gottman in the 1990s shows that mere perspective-taking is an ineffective relationship tool. As Vorauer and Sucharyna explain it in a 2012 American Psychological Association paper, perspective-takers overestimate their own transparency in regard to their values, preferences, traits, and feelings. They lose self-evaluation acuity—develop more blind spots—and create more discrepancies between their own and their partners' experience of their exchanges. This prompts more negative responses, leaving both dissatisfied. However, with binocular vision, you never give up awareness of your own perspective; you *add* to it, through a deeper understanding of your partner's.

If you find yourself stuck in the Toddler brain, simply refrain from any judgments until you can shift to the Adult brain and employ binocular vision.

If your relationship slips easily into blame, denial, and avoidance, you will need *practice* to develop habits of binocular vision. The following can help.

Binocular vision exercise:

When I feel sad, my partner probably feels:

_____

When I feel anxious, my partner probably feels:

_____

When I feel trapped, my partner probably feels:

_____

Try this exercise with every dispute and troublesome disagreement you've had with your partner. As you widen your perspective, you strengthen the Adult brain, feel better, and begin to build a powerful love.

Binocular Vision Dynamics

Recall that the dynamics of an interaction include the movement or exchanges between the parties—what *both* parties do, say, think, and feel, whether proactive or reactive to each other. The trouble is, the Toddler brain is hypersensitive to what our partners do when emotionally aroused, but is not sensitive at all to what *we* do. Perspectives become narrow, rigid, and resistant to any feedback that mitigates negative assumptions. The inevitable result is blind spots and being locked into monocular vision. I discussed blind spots in the chapter on intimate relationship dynamics. I'll address them now because they can serve as impediments to binocular vision.

There's no shame in having blind spots. We can't really help it. Only a tiny proportion of brain cells seem to originate objective analysis of our own demeanor and behavior. Unfortunately, that part receives practically no synaptic activation during emotional arousal. Our brains are simply not wired for accurate self-evaluation during emotional arousal.

What's more, negative arousal keeps us hyperfocused on a perceived threat and practically impervious to information that might mitigate the threat. That is how the people you love can seem like sabertooth tigers or selfish bastards when you're angry or resentful.

Once again let me point out that it's absolutely imperative to identify your blind spots, own them without being defensive, and adjust your behavior to compensate for them. The best strategy uses the reactions of your partner as a system of rear- and side-view mirrors. If you believe that your partner is *attacking you*, ask yourself if you're devaluing him or her, at least in your head. If you think your partner is *being selfish*, ask yourself if you're coming off selfishly. If you suspect that your partner is *condescending, or disrespectful*, ask yourself if you are being respectful and open to his or her perspective. If you guess that your partner is *devoid of compassion and caring*, ask yourself if you are compassionate and caring at that moment.

How Is My Partner Perceiving *Me* at This Moment?

Blind spots give us a false sense of how we come off to our partners. If we think we're right, our blind spots make us falsely believe that we seem to be rational and credible to our partners. Remember Sal, who was understandably distraught about the family's overdrawn checkbook?

"This is the third time I've asked you to look at the account balance before you write a check! We're overdrawn again!"

I asked Sal how he believed his wife perceived him at the moment he made this statement. Initially he said:

"She knows that I'm right and she screwed up."

"If she simply believed that you're right, she would be apologetic. But you said she was furious, so what was she responding to that made her so upset? How was she perceiving you?"

He sighed deeply, finally getting it. "She saw me as angry and controlling."

"What else?"

"A bully, who doesn't care about how she feels."

"Do you want her to perceive you that way?"

"No, that's wrong, she shouldn't see me that way, I'm right."

"Will proving you're right change the perception that you're an angry, controlling bully who doesn't care how she feels?"

"No."

"How can you help her see you as you really are, concerned about her well-being and that of your children?"

"Well, I guess I have to make it about the well-being of our family, because she wants that, too, and not focus on the mistake. And not imply that's she lazy, irresponsible, or doing it on purpose."

To illustrate how blind spots keep us trapped in the Toddler brain, consider the classic standoff:

"If you loved me you would go to my friend's house for dinner."

"If you loved me you wouldn't ask me to go to your friend's house for dinner, because you know I don't get along with her husband."

Both partners are unaware that they appear selfish to each other. Here's how the same interaction from binocular vision might go:

"I know it's uncomfortable for you to go to my friend's house for dinner. But she's my best friend, and she'd be really hurt if we didn't go. She has a hard time, too, with her husband's rudeness, and that's why I want to show support for her. Is there anything I can do to make it more comfortable for you?"

"I know she's your best friend, and I can imagine that it's hard for her living with him. How about if you sit next to me and rub my hand if he starts to get obnoxious."

This was a great strategy, which my clients came up with on their own. Research shows that holding hands calms jittery neurons in the brain. Regardless of what this couple decided—

to go to dinner or not go—they were drawn together by a deeper understanding in the Adult brain, rather than torn apart in Toddler-brain power struggles.

Say It Out Loud

Just saying the words "binocular vision" can activate the Adult brain, because only in the Adult brain can we take other people's perspectives.

Say it out loud:

"Binocular vision."

"Binocular vision."

"Binocular vision."

Train yourself to think in terms of binocular vision:

"I think this, what do you think? I feel this way, how do you feel? I want this, what do you want? This seems fair to me, does it seem fair to you?"

One thing's for sure, practicing binocular vision will free you from the Toddler-brain illusion of sameness and reveal how different you are from your partner. Appreciation and tolerance of differences, which can only be accomplished in the Adult brain, are crucial to the health of love relationships, as we'll see in the next chapter.

CHAPTER TWELVE

Adults in Love Respect Individuality and Honor Differences

The Toddler brain has almost no patience with differences in temperament, ideas, tastes, and preferences. Any assertion of a partner's individuality is likely to cause a level of discomfort intolerable to the Toddler brain.

As we have seen, most of the discomfort that toddlers experience is physiological (hungry, tired, thirsty), but a good portion results from their struggles with the Grand Human Contradiction. Differences are threatening to the underdeveloped sense of autonomy in the Toddler brain, while the individuality of loved ones feels like rejection. At the first hint of discomfort, we're likely to devalue our partners and disrespect their differences, as long as we're in the Toddler brain. Though it harms the relationship, the adrenaline that comes from the act of devaluing temporarily increases energy and a sense of autonomy, while suppressing the individuality of the partner.

"Individuality" is a catch-all term for those qualities that make a person different from everyone else. These are personality traits (such as sociability, conscientiousness, agreeableness, extraversion), temperament (shy, uninhibited), tastes, preferences, and behavioral tendencies (I like this, prefer that, and usually behave this way), accumulated past experience, and core vulnerabilities (the painful feelings we most try to avoid). It also includes what we commonly call "character," which rises from fidelity to (or violation of) personal and social values:

"She's honest, he's loyal. He's selfish, she's selfless. She's conservative, he's liberal."

In the Toddler brain, individuality is primarily negative and reactive: "No! (I don't know who I am, but I know who I'm not.) I'm not whatever you want!" In the Adult brain, it's mostly positive and proactive: "I am," for example, "soft-spoken, decisive, considerate, compassionate, kind, loving, supportive, fair, flexible, strong, and I will act on no behavior impulses that are inconsistent with those qualities."

Respect for differences in love relationships is so important that we need to consider each dimension of individuality in a little more detail.

Personality traits are the source of much chauvinism in love relationships. If I'm sociable and you're not, I might take it personally if you don't want to visit friends, because you *should* want to visit friends. You'll be offended that I don't want to stay home with you, because I *should* want to stay home with you.

Temperament has many components that greatly influence tastes, preferences, choices, and decision making. In a shorthand way of looking at it, your temperament is your innate emotional tone—what it feels like to be you.

In its most fundamental aspects, temperament changes little over a lifetime; temperamental classifications of infants tend to persist into old age. But this can be misleading, as individual strategies to manage temperamental traits create much of the variance we see in people. Shy children, for example, can grow up to make a living in areas like politics or public speaking. They remain fundamentally shy but are able to overcome temperamental inhibitions through practice of social skills. They will never be the life of the party, but they can learn to enjoy the life of the party; they won't tell jokes or amusing stories, but they can share in laughter at them.

If you think your partner doesn't get you or doesn't get the "real" you, it may well be that you're caught in a dance of Toddler-brain reactivity ("No! Mine!"), which distorts your temperamental qualities by making them seem more extreme.

For example, if you're mellow and laid-back, your partner is probably vigilant and meticulous. It's likely that you've become mellower to try to keep the tension in the house at a minimum, which caused your partner to become more meticulous to compensate.

The dimension of temperament most likely to be exaggerated (and misinterpreted) is *intensity*. Broadly speaking, people with high innate energy have higher metabolic rates, are more inclined to action than reflection, apply themselves equally to a wide variety of tasks, and prefer some kind of external structure to guide their higher levels of energy. In extreme cases, they're perfectionists. Those with lower energy levels tend to have a slower metabolism, think before acting (they like to mull things over), and prefer a looser external structure, so they can decide where to invest their more limited energy. They put most of their energy into just a few areas and do the rest on autopilot.

Higher-intensity temperaments usually present with higher levels of anxiety. Conflicts in intimate relationships tend to cluster around anxiety regulation. What lowers anxiety in one may raise it in the other. One focuses on details, while the other attends to the big picture; one is more organized, orderly, punctual, and rigid, while the other feels oppressed by the order and rigidity imposed by the other. One is unable to feel at ease if something is out of place, while the other finds it too distracting to stop what he or she is doing to put things in their place. For some, a paper clip lying loose on the desk raises anxiety to the point where concentration seems impossible. But for those sitting next to them, having to stop what they're doing to put the paper clip in its holder raises anxiety to the point where concentration seems unattainable.

Research indicates that "opposites attract" is an overstatement. We don't look for complete opposites. Rather, we're drawn to people with *moderate* differences in temperament, looking for potential partners who "fill in our gaps," as a popular movie character put it. For instance, high-intensity people want partners they can relax with, whereas low-intensity folks are attracted to those who energize them. (You bring me up, I calm you down, and we meet in the middle.) Highly organized people admire the spontaneity and tendency to "think outside the box" of their less organized potential partners, who, in turn, enjoy the stability and "feet-on-the-ground" qualities of their potential partners.

Although we're not attracted to complete opposites, we seem to become opposites the longer we live together. Over time, differences in emotional tone trigger retreat to the Toddler brain, thereby widening the moderate differences that first attracted us. For instance, anxiety in the more intense partner elevates in response to the carefree demeanor of the other:

"He (she) doesn't worry about anything! If I don't keep pushing, and keep so many balls in the air, everything will fall apart!"

The more laid-back partner responds to the elevated anxiety of the other by trying to "let go" or "back off, because things are getting so uptight." The more anxious the one becomes, the more "laid-back" the other seems. In their Toddler brains, one seems high-strung and controlling, whereas the other seems irresponsible or disengaged. The same qualities that attract partners dissolve in a fog of resentment when Toddler-brain reactivity makes it seem like you got more than you bargained for. One complains:

"I wanted somebody energetic, not bouncing off the damn walls! Just calm down!"

And the other counters:

"I wanted someone mellow, not dead! Get up and do something!"

In the Toddler brain, temperamental differences feel like betrayal:

"You used to love me for this quality, and now you criticize me about it."

"You told me you loved me, but you can't accept me for who I am."

Because they're caught in a relentless competition about whose temperament will prevail, all their arguments take the form of:

"You have to be like me!"

Interestingly, when couples separate, they usually revert to their temperamental set-point before they started fighting. When no longer pushed to extremes by reacting to each other, the "sloppy" person becomes neater, while the "compulsively neat" person grows more relaxed. The disorganized partner becomes more orderly, while the highly organized person can once again tolerate a paper clip out of its holder.

Though criticism is always worse than feedback (Chapter Four), criticism of temperamental differences feels the most personal. It causes resentment and depression in the one being criticized while increasing resentment, anxiety, and frustration in the one who does the criticism.

You can tell if you're in a dispute about temperament if the following are present:

- Your partner seems "wrong" in the way he or she perceives things
- Your partner doesn't really get why you're annoyed
- One or both of you are convinced that your way is the *only right way*

The classic temperamental conflict that affects most people who live together is the "neat/messy dilemma." It's a dilemma because you can't even describe the conflict without appearing to take sides. One partner prefers a high level of neatness or orderliness in the home, while the other wants it to appear "lived-in, like people can actually relax there," as one of my clients put it. Here's how it typically plays out in the Toddler brain:

"You know I can't stand a messy house. Decent people don't live like this."

"Lots of decent people live like this. Most people aren't so compulsive and controlling. Can't you just let me relax for a minute?"

Arguing about what most people will do, like opposing lawyers in a trial, is never going to work in an intimate relationship. The superficial reason is that there's no Neatness Police to settle our differences. More to the point, couples don't really fight about the way the house looks; they fight about the belief that their partners don't care how they feel. In the Adult brain, we don't assume that our partners *should* think and act the way we do. Rather, we negotiate about specific behaviors with respect and value, acknowledging our temperamental bias. Here's how such a negotiation might sound in the Adult brain:

"I know I'm a little rigid on this, but it really gets to me when things are piled on the counter instead of put away. I know you don't want me to be anxious, and I don't want you to feel controlled. What can we do so we can both feel more comfortable in our house?"

"I don't leave stuff on the counter to upset you, it's just not on my radar screen because it's not that important to me. But you're important to me, so I'll try to remember to put things away."

"If you make an effort to remember, I won't hassle you when you really do forget."

With temperamental differences, both partners must come out of their comfort zone a little, motivated by compassion and kindness for each other. Notice that the exchange above focused on common values—each other's well-being—rather than temporary feelings.

Core vulnerabilities are those things that hurt the most, for which we have the least tolerance and the most rigid coping mechanisms. Everyone has a "core" vulnerability that is worse than any other he or she might have. These "sore spots" are activated by a lesser stimulus than other vulnerabilities. They last longer and often cause flashbacks—involuntary revisiting of vulnerable or painful states—for hours, days, weeks, or months afterwards. For example, consider the different experience of fear between Mark, whose core vulnerability is shame, and Sarah, whose core vulnerability is fear. Sarah can startle at a sudden loud noise, whereas it would take an explosion to invoke the same level of fear in Mark. The experience may flash back a few times in the course of the day for Sarah, whereas Mark will quickly forget about it.

On the other hand, Mark would find getting cut off by a driver on the highway humiliating, react to it with irritation or a depressed mood for quite a while, and think about it off and on throughout the day. Sarah would find the cut-off mildly unpleasant for a minute or two, then quickly forget about it.

The experience of the lesser vulnerability will trigger the core vulnerability in both the fear- and shame-avoidant. For instance, for Sarah, the experience of shame is likely to trigger a deeper and more dreadful fear of isolation, harm, or deprivation: "If I fail, no one will help, love, or comfort me. I'll lose my home and everything I love."

For Mark, fear will trigger a deeper and more loathsome sense of failure and inadequacy: "If I give in to fear, I'll feel like a failure or a coward; I won't be able to help, love, or comfort myself, and I won't want anyone else's help, love, or comfort." Closeness seems to amplify the discomfort of the shame-avoidant. The root of the word "shame" means to cover or hide. When people get too close, the vulnerability becomes more difficult to hide. The cant of the shame-avoidant partner is, "I don't want to talk about it. Just leave me alone"

When the fear-driven fail at work, they want more closeness in their relationships—closeness lowers fear. When the shame-avoidant fail at work, they're likely to get irritable (drive their partners away) or withdraw, preferring to be left alone and drink more alcohol.

People whose core vulnerability is fear of harm, isolation, or deprivation will accept shame, even humiliation if they have to, in order to feel safe, secure, or connected, or at least to avoid feeling isolated. He or she will stay with a critical or even an abusive partner who makes a lot of money or offers protection from outside threats or intermittently allays feelings of isolation. People whose core vulnerability is shame will risk harm, resources, and relationships to feel successful, or at least to avoid feeling like a failure or a coward. They'll respond to a mugging with fantasies of revenge, which, if enacted, would put them in greater harm's way.

Core vulnerabilities shape how we perceive the world. Those whose core vulnerability is fear look at the world very differently from those whose core vulnerability is shame. Fearful people seek to build alliances—there's strength in numbers, which tends to make them more sensitive to the emotional states of others. Those whose core vulnerability is shame try to project an aura of competence or mastery and seek status to allay feelings of inadequacy. This can make them less sensitive to the emotional states of others.

Past experience is the hardest element of individuality to detect, much less appreciate. We have no way of knowing the effects of what our partners experience in the course of the day, the week, the year, or their lives. When we think we know, we're more likely projecting the effects of our own experience onto them, and judging them by how we would respond with similar experiences. One thing's for sure, unless you marry your brother or sister, your partner will bring very different experiences to your interactions.

Emotional meaning would be different even if you did marry your brother or sister. That's because the emotional meaning people give to their experience is determined by other aspects of individuality, temperament, and vulnerability, as well as physiological states, hormone levels, and emotion regulation skill, all of which are likely to vary in families.

Never assume that your partner has the same experience as you, even if you're involved in the same events at the same time. The meaning partners give to seemingly common experiences is the most fertile ground for Toddler-brain standoffs. Once again, the scientific evidence suggests that when emotionally aroused, we're more likely to project how we feel onto others than to read their feelings accurately. At best, we misunderstand people to some degree when trying to identify with their experience, as it necessarily differs from our own. In the Toddler brain, the way *we* would respond becomes the gold standard of appropriateness:

"I can't empathize with you, because I wouldn't be afraid of someone yelling. There's nothing to be afraid of!"

"I wouldn't be ashamed to ask for a raise that would help our family, because I wouldn't feel like a failure if the boss said no. Grow up already!"

Think of how often you've heard statements like:

"I would never have done what he did."

"How could she possibly feel that way?"

"I just don't get how they could have reacted like they did."

These types of statements result from Toddler-brain intolerance of the differences in emotional meaning that people give to seemingly common experiences.

Consider the topic that most often elicits Toddler-brain standoffs in relationships: acquiring money and spending it. The primary reason that most couples have conflicts about money is that it means something different to each partner. To many people, money represents security and safety. To others it means power and influence. To some it means cold calculation. For others it enables expression of heartfelt generosity or compassion or love. For still others, spending money is a measure of personal worthiness. Any attempt at negotiation between intimate partners about money is certain to make matters worse, if the different emotional meanings the partners give to it are not respected.

For example, I once treated a couple on a national TV show. Eleanor got furious when the first thing Terry said when he saw that she had gotten a new haircut was, "How much did it cost?"

For Terry, the cost of the haircut was a matter of balancing the checkbook. Because it plugged into his provider anxiety (he didn't feel he made as much money as the family needed), his question about the cost had more emotional intensity than he realized. For Eleanor, Terry's question about cost implied, as she tearfully put it, once we worked through the anger, that she wasn't "worth the money."

At the end of treatment, Terry *owned* his provider anxiety without blaming it on Eleanor, who, in turn, no longer ridiculed him about it as they negotiated beyond it. He assured her that she was *worth* everything that the richest person on the planet could buy, and if they had the resources, they wouldn't have to worry about the checkbook. (Money should never be about worthiness; it's only about resources.) Most of the time, the provider anxiety that underlies many disputes about money are not about the cost of specific items so much as an irrational fear of hemorrhaging—"If you spend this, what next, we'll bleed to death!" To alleviate the fear of hemorrhaging, Terry and Eleanor came up with a discretionary budget that was agreeable to both of them. No particular expenditure would be mentioned by either, as long as they stayed within the discretionary budget. Because they appreciated the differences in the meaning they each gave to money, they were able to negotiate successfully about their spending, with neither feeling devalued or manipulated.

The important point about differences is that one element of individuality is not inherently better than the other, as long as none violates deeper values. Nobody has a license to have his or her way of managing individual temperament, core vulnerability, past experience, or emotional meaning prevail over anyone else's. No one has the right to say that because I feel a certain way about something, you have to feel that way, too.

Though not always easy, the effort it takes to appreciate differences in temperament, vulnerabilities, experience, and emotional meaning adds depth and dynamism to love relationships. It makes life more interesting and vital.

Disagreements in the Adult Brain

Believe it or not, research on happy relationships shows that they feature more disagreements than unhappy (Toddler-brain) relationships. The idea that happy partners agree about everything is a complete myth. The big difference between the happy and the unhappy is not the frequency of disagreements but tolerance of differences. Happy partners appreciate their different perspectives, or at least tolerate them. Unhappy couples resent their differences.

Many years ago I participated in a study of the variables that distinguish happy from unhappy couples. (The classifications were determined by both partners scoring similarly high or low on a number of marital satisfaction measures.) As a follow-up, we showed several couples from each group a popular movie that its promoters identified as a "chick flick"—one that marketing research indicated would appeal to women but not to men. After the film, we interviewed each couple, making a point at the outset of asking the man how he liked the movie.

The first man we interviewed was from the happy group. He said something like:

"It was okay, but nothing much really happened, not much of a plot."

He had barely stopped speaking when his wife enthusiastically described the film's depiction of a mother-daughter relationship. It started out conflicted, went through an emotional crisis, and ended up in amelioration. The woman's husband was interested in what she described. He hadn't noticed the mother-daughter theme and appreciated that she pointed it out to him, as it helped him think better of the movie in retrospect. He paused a bit and then added:

"I still wish there had been a little more action, though."

A husband from the unhappily married group said pretty much the same thing that his happily married counterpart initially reported—the movie was boring, without much action. The wife reported, when asked, that she didn't like it either. Because she made the appraisal without conviction, we asked her again, later in the interview, pointing out that the other women we interviewed seemed to like some things about the movie. But she repeated, with even less conviction, that she didn't like it. At the end of the interview, we told her that we had videotaped the audience as they viewed the film, and she seemed to be watching with interest. She replied, again without a lot of enthusiasm:

"Well, I did like the relationship between the mother and daughter . . ."

She went on to describe the same relationship dynamic portrayed in the film that most of the women in the happily married group cited. But while she was speaking, her husband was shaking his head, as if embarrassed and disgusted.

"That would be like you to like a mindless movie like that."

These contrasting interviews help explain the empirical finding that happily married couples have more disagreements than unhappily married couples. On paper, the happily married couple disagreed about the movie. The disagreement enriched the experience of both—the wife related her experience in a way that led to post hoc appreciation by her husband. Yet he didn't change his overall opinion about the movie. In other words, they maintained a balance between autonomy and connection. On paper, the unhappily married couple agreed about the movie, but only because disagreement would have led to criticism or rejection, forcing a Toddler-brain choice between autonomy and connection.

Appreciate, Tolerate, Negotiate

Here's an important *Power love* motto:

Appreciate as many individual differences as you can, and tolerate the ones you can't appreciate.

Appreciation is opening your heart and mind to certain qualities of other people or things. For example, when I appreciate how loving you are, your fine work, or your thoughtful gestures, I am enhanced, that is, I become a better person as long as I appreciate you. (This is why appreciating and being appreciated are so appealing in relationships: both parties become better people.) What's more, my appreciation of you has expansive benefit, helping me to appreciate the beauty of the sunset, the drama of the painting, or the excitement of the movie or play.

What we cannot appreciate, we must tolerate. Tolerance is the ability to accept other people's opinions, emotional states, and behaviors that differ from ours.

As we saw in Part I, the high emotional reactivity of the Toddler brain makes partners particularly intolerant of negative emotions and opposing ideas in each other, which they perceive as threats to autonomy or connection. Without tolerance, negotiation can easily deteriorate into pleading, demanding, or coercing.

Tolerance is something the brain does automatically when we don't short-circuit the process through Toddler-brain blame. Without blame, emotional response diminishes over time as conditions become familiar. That's how the bad gets bearable and people adapt to poverty, prisons, air raids, and concentration camps.

The Tolerance Scale below, filled out weekly for the next several weeks, will help you appreciate the importance of tolerance in building a *Power love*. Reading the statements and assigning a value to them retrains the brain to become more tolerant in your relationship.

TOLERANCE SCALE		
Indicate the current level of tolerance in your relationship, as well as the level you would like to reach in the future, using this scale: 2 = high tolerance 1 = mild tolerance 0 = no tolerance		
My partner's tolerance of me when:	**Now**	**Goal**
I am hyper and my partner is calm or vice versa		
I am serious and my partner is joking or vice versa		
I am neat and my partner is messy or vice versa		

My partner's tolerance of me when:	Now	Goal
I want to start on a joint project and my partner wants to do more research or vice versa		
I want to plan and my partner wants to be spontaneous or vice versa		
I am punctual and my partner is not or vice versa		
I am worried and my partner is distracted or vice versa		
I want details and my partner stays focused on the "big picture" or vice versa		
I want to express feelings and my partner wants to chill out or vice versa		
I am talky and my partner is quiet or vice versa		
Soft background music helps me concentrate, but my partner wants absolute quiet or vice versa		
I have a strong opinion or preference that my partner disagrees with or vice versa		
I am interested in something and my partner is bored or vice versa		
I am romantic and my partner is not or vice versa		

Note: Of course, there are limits to tolerance. We must never tolerate behavior that violates core values, including any behavior that is deceitful or dishonest. Neither can we tolerate abuse—behavior intended to make you feel bad about yourself so you will do what your partner wants.

Soar Above the Discomfort That Stirs Intolerance

The low tolerance of discomfort in the Toddler brain practically guarantees blame, denial, and avoidance.

"You're talking too loudly (or too softly)."

"Why can't you ever consider who else is in the room when you make that noise?"

"Don't sneak up on me; make some noise when you come into the room."

The tragedy of blame is that it turns benign issues into relationship problems. In reality, most triggers of uncomfortable states are *physiological*, with *no* psychological or relationship meaning. For instance, the most misunderstood of uncomfortable feelings are tension and irritability. Variations in day-by-day tension and irritability come from general immune system functioning and tissue inflammation. These in turn are influenced by the ways we sleep, eat, drink, and exercise, as well as fluctuations in room and outdoor temperature and from how the body metabolizes hormones like oxytocin, testosterone, estrogen, and norepinephrine. In terms of volatility, the greatest fluctuations are caused by the hormones epinephrine and cortisol. Elevated levels of these have many causes, ranging from general stress to loud noises to abrupt environmental changes.

The reason we give psychological meaning to physiological sensations goes beyond the still-pervasive influence of Freud and early-twentieth-century psychiatrists who held that every feeling meant something. It's really a matter of how the brain works.

A primary function of the prefrontal cortex is to interpret and explain experience. The inability to understand negative experience is anxiety-provoking and can be overwhelming:

"My God, why is this happening to me?"

To keep anxiety manageable, we would rather have a bad explanation than no explanation at all. I would rather think that I feel bad because I'm a loser (or my coworkers are dicks, my congressman is corrupt, or my partner is selfish) than have no idea why I feel bad. When it comes to pain and discomfort, the human brain craves explanation more than truth.

Of course, bad explanations stimulate more alarms in the Toddler brain, which responds with more blame, denial, or avoidance. Soon the problems of relationships seem to be problems of character.

For example, this is how a married couple described each other on their first day of treatment:

"He's a selfish, passive-aggressive, irresponsible, destructive, lazy, abusive, bulldozing, spoiled-brat crybaby."

Of course, her husband had a different take. He described her this way:

"She's controlling, unreasonable, and rejecting; you can't talk to her about anything without her being verbally demeaning and abusive; you just have to stay away from her."

Believe it or not, they reached this level of contempt by blaming physically caused irritability on each other. Once they understood that their discomfort was mostly physical in origin and stopped blaming it on each other, their relationship improved dramatically. This revelatory knowledge freed them to develop habits of responding to discomfort in ways that made them feel more comfortable and valuable. Irritability became a signal to connect through gentle eye contact, touch, embrace, or kiss.

Although science does not yet indicate that all bad feelings are biological in origin, biological factors should always be ruled out first. If you want a *Power love*, strive to test your explanation of negative feelings in a quasi-scientific manner. Here are examples:

Biological Explanation: "My partner is not irritating me; I'm irritable because I stayed up too late or drank too much or haven't exercised."

Test: Sleep more or drink less or exercise consistently, and see if the irritability persists.

Biological Explanation: "I got furious at my partner for criticizing my driving. I blamed her for the enormous spike in adrenaline and cortisol in my bloodstream, which I experienced when that other car abruptly cut into my cone of perception (or when she gasped in fear), stimulating a threat response."

Test: Instead of blaming her for the discomfort, realize that it was caused by a natural reaction to an abrupt change in the environment that had life-threatening potential. (Blame perpetuates the sense of threat and keeps the adrenaline and cortisol flowing.)

Without blame, you should return to your normal self in a few minutes, as adrenaline and cortisol levels recede. Then you might notice that your partner's startle was involuntary, and her fear is more likely to invoke compassion and the desire to protect. You can also channel the heightened focus provided by the adrenaline onto a problem at work or home that's been bothering you. It's like a free Grande at Starbucks. Don't waste it on anger.

To sum up, most of what the Toddler brain wants to blame, deny, or avoid are the results of individual differences in personality traits, temperament, core vulnerability, past experience, and emotional meaning. The Adult brain can learn to appreciate, or at least tolerate, most of these. The Adult brain uses discomfort as motivation to improve, appreciate, connect, or protect. The next chapter shows how to develop habits of Adult-brain coping that will make it easier to stay in the profoundest part of the brain under any kind of stress.

CHAPTER THIRTEEN

Developing Adult-Brain Habits

Insight about the interplay of the Toddler and Adult brains, along with skills to switch from the former to the latter, are the foundation of *Power love*. However, as long as Toddler-brain coping mechanisms remain on the level of unconscious habits, they can strike any time that stress is high and physical resources are low. This chapter offers a technique to change emotional habits.

I wish I could say that it's easier, but the only way to change an emotional habit is to develop a new one that is incompatible with the old. To change the Toddler-brain impulse to blame, deny, or avoid, we have to recondition the brain to respond with improve, appreciate, connect, or protect. About 12 years ago, I developed a habit-changing technique for my clinical practice, called **TIP**.[1]

The mammalian brain acquires new habits only by repetition, which means we must *practice* new habits of emotion

---

[1] I originally published this technique in *Soar Above: How to Use the Most Profound Part of Your Brain Under Any Kind of Stress.*

regulation. Before I describe what the practice sessions look like, there are a few preliminary steps to consider. The first is to identify the antecedents and triggers of Toddler-brain habits and make a list of specific behaviors that will make you feel valuable whenever you feel devalued. Below is an example.

Antecedents of Toddler-brain habits	Triggers	Adult-brain habits
Hungry, tired, unwell, too much caffeine/alcohol/ sugar, sad, lonely, irritable. Thinking of how people take advantage of me or try to control or disregard me. Thinking of ways to retaliate.	My partner does or says something that I think devalues or disrespects me.	Improve, appreciate, connect, protect. Practice compassion and kindness. She either didn't mean to devalue me or she's feeling devalued herself.

Once you've completed the above, you're ready to use **TIP**. The steps are:

Think repeatedly about the desired change and, if you journal, write about it.

Imagine what you will do to make the change (overcoming possible barriers).

Practice in simulated stress and in real life the specific behaviors likely to lead to the desired change.

Although individuals vary in the number of repetitions it takes to form a habit, my clinical experience is that about 12 repetitions of **TIP** per day will form the habit. Don't gasp in horror about your busy schedule; the practice sessions are only a couple of minutes each, spread throughout the day.

Anything you have to do often works best with a regimen of doing it at the same time every day. (If you have trouble sticking to a goal of exercising regularly, it's probably because you try to do it at different times.) Practicing at the same time every day establishes a routine, which makes it easier to remember—it feels not quite right if you don't do it.

Practice Regimen

To ensure that the new habit will generalize to all physical and mental states, spread out the 12 sessions across the day. A transitional time occurs when you stop doing one thing and start doing another. The suggested regimen below covers transitional times, which are the most likely to produce negative emotions. Adapt it to fit your schedule.

As you get out of bed

Just before you leave the house

Just before you enter the workplace

At morning break time

At lunch time

At afternoon break time

Just before you leave work

Just before you go into the house

Just before dinner

Just after dinner

While preparing for bed

At bedtime

Desired change	Thoughts & writing	Imagining	Practice
When I feel devalued, I will appreciate the benefits my partner adds to my life.	When she says that I'm selfish, I will recognize that she feels hurt and devalued, and I will let her know that I care.	I feel guilty about having been selfish in the past, but caring about my partner and feeling connected to her is more important, so I will focus on what is most important.	I will ask her to talk about times when she thought I was selfish, and I will practice a compassionate response.

It's advisable to begin with a habit you want to change in work or social contexts, before applying the technique to the more complicated domain of disputes with loved ones. The optimal way to habituate any skill set is to start with relatively low stress and gradually increase the stress as the steps become familiar. You don't learn to swim in the ocean in a storm or to drive a truck on a highway in heavy traffic.

If it sounds like a lot of work to develop Adult-brain habits, it is. But I believe it's the only way to reverse the pervasive effects of Toddler-brain habits, which, most of the time, lead to failure and pain.

Forming Habits to Increase Core Value

A lifetime of Toddler-brain habits can destabilize self-value. When self-value declines, we tend to use the low-grade adrenaline of resentment or anger to substitute temporary feelings of power and confidence for genuine self-value. The adrenaline makes us feel, however temporarily, that we're better than other people and thereby locks us in the Toddler brain. Habits that raise self-value can undo the harm by allowing us to feel okay without devaluing anyone else.

First identify a repertoire of thoughts and behaviors that make you feel more valuable. These will be practiced in association with your vulnerable states, to form beneficial habits. The goal is to automatically do something that will make you feel more valuable when you feel devalued.

Think about times in the past when you felt more valuable. Once again, value-enhancing behaviors tend to fall into four general categories: *improve, appreciate, connect,* and *protect.*

Improve example: Most people are able to improve situations in love relationships, at least a little, when they listen attentively to their partners during disagreements. Instead of trying to refute their partners, they provide more information. Listening and augmenting, instead of refuting or devaluing, tends to make us feel more valuable and our partners more valued. The corrective behavior in this example is *listening without contradicting,* which you would practice when you felt devalued.

My *improve* behaviors:

1. _____

2. _____

3. _____

Appreciate example: My wife stayed up with me all night in the emergency room of the hospital after I suffered a kidney stone attack. The corrective behavior in this example is *imagining her fighting off exhaustion because she didn't want me to be alone.*

My *appreciate* behaviors:

1. _____

2. _____

3. _____

Connect example: When people are angry, they are almost always trying to avoid feeling hurt or vulnerable. If I sympathize with my partner's hurt or vulnerability, I'll likely experience compassion and a motivation to help, which will make me feel more valuable and my partner feel more valued. The corrective behavior in this example is *focus on your partner's hurt or vulnerability and try to help, even when he or she is angry at me.*

My *connect* behaviors:

1. _____

2. _____

3. _____

Protect example: I imagine my response to a stranger who said or did the most hurtful thing that I have ever said or done to my partner. The corrective behavior in this example is *imagine myself protecting the well-being of my partner—reassuring and encouraging.*

My *protect* behaviors:

1. _____

2. _____

3. _____

To develop habits of choosing value over power, use **TIP**:

Think repeatedly about the desired change and, if you journal, write about it ("When my partner says I'm selfish, I will allow myself to care that he or she is hurt and show that I care.")

Imagine in detail how to overcome any barriers (usually guilt, shame, anxiety) to the desired change ("I feel guilty about having been selfish in the past, but caring about my partner and feeling connected is more important, so I will try to focus on what is most important to me.")

Practice in simulated stress and in real life the specific behaviors likely to lead to the desired change.

"Practice in simulated stress" means asking your partner to deliberately provoke you with various comments and behaviors, which in the past were followed by angry outbursts—for example, voicing an intention to buy something desired but not, in your opinion, needed. (The practice incidents should be *varied* to achieve a generalized effect, rather than to just desensitize one or two specific provocations.)

Set aside three minutes for each practice session. When you're apart, your partner can text the provocative remarks. After each practice session, make a mental note of how much more valuable the new behavior makes you feel, compared to the old response of anger or aggression.

Practice associating the "improve, appreciate, connect, protect" behaviors you described above with feelings of diminished value. It takes about 12 repetitions per day for about six weeks to form the new habit.

Make a list of the three most recent incidents when you reacted in violation of your deeper values. Do not provide context or descriptions of the triggers.

1. _____

2. _____

3. _____

Identify the antecedents of the hurtful behavior—what *you* were thinking, feeling, and doing—as well as the state of your physical resources (hungry, tired, thirsty, having consumed more than two drinks or more than two cups of coffee, or having eaten too much sugar) immediately before the infraction:

Antecedent of behaviors:

1. _____

2. _____

3. _____

Practice associating the vulnerable states that led to the undesired behavior with the "improve, appreciate, connect, or protect" behaviors you identified above.

For a detailed example of the **TIP** process, I'll use my client, Joel. I like to use him as an example because he made so much progress in such a short time. I've written about him before and he has accompanied me on workshops to demonstrate the technique.

At first, the hardest part for Joel, as for most of my clients, was developing a repertoire of valuing behaviors. (People who retreat to the Toddler brain under stress simply do not know how to make themselves feel valuable.) Not coincidentally, valuing behaviors fall into four categories: *improve*, *appreciate*, *connect*, and *protect*.

Under *improve*, Joel described how he responded to his boss's rude behavior by recognizing that the company was losing money. He sympathized with his boss, who felt responsible for the losses. Although he couldn't change his boss's behavior, the shift in attitude definitely improved his experience. For *appreciate*, he recalled pulling off the road on his commute to work to watch the sunrise. For *connect*, he wrote about his special efforts to engage with his wife, Marnie, realizing that she sometimes felt isolated due to his natural introversion and, more importantly, his history of Toddler-brain sulking. For *protect*, he remembered spending a Saturday rescuing stray cats for the local pet adoption agency. Once he had these four, he was able to come up with a whole repertoire of valuing behaviors that he could do or imagine when he felt devalued.

The Toddler-brain habit Joel most wanted to change was lashing out at his wife. Although he never overtly threatened his family, his anger sometimes frightened his wife and kids. It takes only a couple of incidents of fear to begin walking on eggshells; you never know when something might "set him off," as Marnie put it. Joel designed his practice sessions to correct this terrible Toddler-brain habit. He wrote about several times he felt devalued at home. These were mostly small ego offenses, such as Marnie not listening to him when she was busy or when she complained about him not helping with their two kids. The antecedents were usually irritability from sleep deprivation and feeling stressed from long hours at work. He worked into the night at a demanding job.

For the actual practice sessions, Joel imagined that the antecedents and triggers were happening now. He imagined himself understanding that his tiredness was not Marnie's fault. (If you don't blame irritability on anyone, it doesn't last very long.) He imagined understanding that she was busy and appreciating how hard she works around the house. He imagined protecting her by offering to help with whatever she was doing, and connecting with her through touch or in his imagination, if she was unavailable for touch at that moment.

He repeated the association of feeling devalued with the corrective behaviors, 12 times per day, until the association became automatic—about six weeks. To simulate the stress of actual interactions, he arranged a couple of practice sessions with Marnie, in which they discussed incidents from the past. Although it lacked the intensity of the actual incidents, the rise in their anxiety from just talking about it was enough to provoke his initial urge to lash out, which he then practiced regulating.

Desired change	Thoughts/ writing	Imagining	Practice
The habit of lashing out at Marnie.	When she seems too busy for me, I'll understand that she's busy and appreciate how hard she works around the house.	I'll make a small gesture of connection, a hug or smile, and ask if I can help her.	I'll ask her what it's like for her when she's busy and I want attention or when she thinks I'm not helping enough around the house.

Not surprisingly, daily practice of behaviors like these created more opportunities to improve, appreciate, connect, and protect, making it easier for Joel to become the person and partner he most wanted to be.

Effort Brings Reward

About 12 years ago, I ran into Joel and Marnie in a grocery store, with their third child, Alex, then five years old. Joel told me that he talked often about **TIP** and still used it to reinforce his new habits whenever he felt stress building. While we were chatting, the little boy wandered off and broke into a run when his pursuing mother called him. Joel then used his deeper and louder voice to get the child's attention. Alex immediately ran back to us, with a look of glee on his face. With his arms extended, he looked straight up at his tall father. He opened and closed his hands six times, as if trying to hypnotize, while calling out, "TIP! TIP! TIP! TIP! TIP! TIP!" Joel looked at his son with as much pleasure as I felt pride in my former client. I couldn't help but appreciate how this sweet little boy could now live an enjoyable life, free of fear.

As you develop new Adult-brain habits, you'll discover that negotiation with your partner becomes easier. Love relationships are all about negotiation, and that is the topic of the next chapter.

CHAPTER FOURTEEN

Power Love Negotiation

I've mentioned several times in these pages that intimate partners respond more to emotional states than to words. The brain reacts emotionally to a speaker before the part that interprets the meaning of the words is activated. If the discussion is emotional, we've already made a judgment about the words before we know what our partners are saying. This is a fact ignored by those who reduce Toddler-brain struggles for autonomy and connection to "communication issues."

Word-choice recommendations are a popular topic in pop psychology because "communication skills" are very easy to teach, not because they improve relationships. The fact is, use of communication techniques in intimate relationships is of little long-term benefit to couples. Some research shows that emphasis on communication techniques *decreases* marital satisfaction, as couples focus on words rather than connection. Observational research by John Gottman and others shows that happily married couples hardly ever use the communication skills taught in self-help books and some therapy sessions. Nevertheless, a question I get all the time from people soliciting relationship advice is:

"What should I say, when he (or she) does (or says) this?"

My pat response is: "Don't worry about what you say; focus on the goal of saying it—on what you want to accomplish—and that will change your emotional demeanor."

Most people claim that the goal of communication is to get cooperation from their partners, and, when pressed, they say that they want cooperation because it makes them feel more connected. Yet they pursue their goals in ways that sound critical, punishing, or manipulating.

Couples are not disconnected because they have poor communication; they have poor communication because they're disconnected.

Think back to the early stages of your relationship, when you felt connected. Chances are you communicated just fine back then. You could talk for hours on end. No doubt you communicated well throughout the relationship, so long as you felt connected. When the periods of connection became fewer and farther between, talking grew more difficult and less successful.

The classic miscommunication in marriage occurs when one partner says something like:

"Honey, we need to talk."

What usually follows is a list of reasons why they're emotionally disconnected, along with lots of Toddler-brain blame for it. No matter how well-meaning, these talks rarely include an expressed desire to connect, which is why they cause more disconnection. Couples fight about the pain of disconnection, which is at the heart of every argument, cold silence, and resentment expressed from the Toddler brain. Words are used to persuade or criticize, not to connect.

Attunement

The primary vehicle of connection in adult relationships is *emotional attunement*, a largely unconscious process by which the emotions (as well as respiratory systems, metabolic rates, and immune functioning) synchronize to those with whom we have emotional bonds. We can consciously attune emotional states through interest and caring—one has to be interested and show care for the other, who, in turn, must be receptive and willing to reciprocate. Otherwise our emotions will attune negatively and most likely trigger Toddler-brain coping mechanisms.

Interest and care, like all emotional states, are conveyed primarily by facial expressions, body language, tone of voice, attitude, and behavior, more than by words. Focusing on communication techniques will get you lost in words and thereby diminish caring and interest in your partner's perspective.

Without interest and care, you'll inadvertently imply that what you want to talk about is more important than your connection. This devalues the connection and makes you both tense and defensive before you can even begin your "talk."

If you need to talk to your partner about something important, make it your goal to connect *before* you try to communicate. Connection occurs with "approach" motivation. That means showing interest, caring, or affection. Instead of starting discussions with complaints, approach your partner with a desire for connection (even if you can't express it at the moment, try to get in touch with it). Develop genuine curiosity about his or her perspective. Keep in mind that she or he is someone you love and value. It's usually a good idea to touch before you speak—gentle touch calms anxiety.

If you don't do the above, anything you say will fail, regardless of the sophistication level of your communication skills. (At best you may feel heard, but not connected.) If you do the above, almost anything you say will likely succeed, regardless of how poorly or awkwardly you put it. The goal of communication in love relationships is not merely to convey information. The long-term goal is to achieve a compassionate and loving connection that goes beyond words.

Where Toddlers Criticize, Adults Negotiate

A burning question in human relationships, at least for those who go to couples counseling, is how to get your partner to do what you want. We've evolved a few tricks over the millennia to be sure, but most of them are not adaptable to complex modern relationships. Here's what most couples try:

1. Coercion (You'll lose approval or status or suffer in some way if you don't do what I want.)

2. Manipulation (I'll trick you into it.)

3. Incentive/bartering (If you do *this* for me, I'll do *that* for you.)

4. Persuasion (Here's why you *should* do what I want, and you *know* I'm right.)

5. Negotiation (Let's find a course of action we can both feel more or less okay about.)

Although choices 1 through 4 can be successful in some types of relationships, they lead to unmitigated disaster in love. *Coercion* can take the form of criticism, demands (intimidation), and devaluing behavior or, in its more covert variations, withholding affection, cooperation, and good will. The clear message is that you will lose something or suffer in some way if you don't do what I want.

Those who use coercive behavior justify their actions by presuming to have superior rights, privileges, intelligence, talents, sensitivity, or entitlements, which automatically prompt negative responses in their partners, regardless of "the facts" of the behavior requests. The unavoidable result of coercion is frequent power struggles, resentment, bitterness, and, eventually, contempt:

"If you don't do this for me, you can pretty much forget about me being nice to your mother."

Manipulation requires a certain amount of deceit or, at best, hidden agendas, which undermine the honesty, openness, and trust necessary for the long-term health of intimate relationships. The mere suspicion of manipulation confounds connection. Discovery of it makes manipulated partners feel like the love they thought they gave was actually stolen. They feel demeaned, but not by the behavior requests themselves, which are often trivial. They feel betrayed by the desire of their loved ones to manipulate them.

Manipulation and coercion often go together when a relationship suffers from a power imbalance, where one party controls the couple's resources and most of its choices. Manipulation is inevitable when power is not shared equally.

Bartering occurs to some extent in the best of relationships, but it carries a high risk. Employed consistently, bartering almost always leads to resentful scorekeeping and the classic impasse:

"I did that for you, so you have to do this for me."

"I thought you did that for me out of love and kindness, not with any strings attached."

Bartering fails in the long run because there are no balance sheets in love.

Persuasion can be accomplished through reasoning, seduction, coaxing, or pleading. While it may succeed occasionally in love relationships, attempts at persuasion too often rise from the same toxic assumptions as coercion—superior rights, privileges, intelligence, talents, sensitivity, or entitlements. With repetition, it has similar negative effects: "Here we go again, you're right and I'm wrong."

Power love negotiation succeeds (or at least never completely fails) because it has built-in respect for both partners. It puts more value on the relationship than on the specific behaviors under negotiation, so that neither partner can lament:

"Getting what you want is more important to you than I am!"

The goal is cooperation. The "spirit of cooperation," to which most intimate partners would subscribe, at least in the abstract, is willing, though not necessarily enthusiastic, support or teamwork for the common good of the relationship. As we've seen, if you want cooperation, you must show value.

Fundamental Rights Are Not Negotiable

The ability to negotiate is one of the most important relationship skills. But negotiation is not possible without fundamental rights guaranteed. Regardless of how factually right you are or how valid your points may be, you cannot successfully negotiate in an intimate relationship if the following *nonnegotiable* rights are not respected:

Unconditional safety—there can be no attempts to harm and no threats to harm, whether implied or explicit.

Freedom from boundary violations—unwanted touching, name-calling, attacks on self-value (trying to make your partner feel bad about himself or herself for not submitting).

Freedom from coercion—forcing your partner to do something against his or her will.

Only with guarantees of safety and freedom from coercion can negotiation begin.

Pre-negotiation

Mental focus amplifies and magnifies. Whatever we focus on becomes more important than what we're not focused on. That neurological fact creates an artificial importance of behaviors under negotiation. To counteract the amplification and magnification effects of mental focus, try the following exercises before you try to negotiate about something that stirs emotions.

The purpose of these exercises is to put you in touch with the deep value you hold for your partner, which must be acknowledged whenever you want cooperation from your partner.

Five things that make me hard to live with:

1. _____

2. _____

3. _____

4. _____

5. _____

Five assets my partner brings to our relationship:

1. _____

2. _____

3. _____

4. _____

5. _____

To successfully negotiate about problems in your relationship, you must see them in a broader context—as *one* color on a larger palette. Some of those colors enrich your life. Some you like, and some you would like changed. It's important to bring the whole palette to a negotiation.

List the behaviors and personal qualities of your loved one that enrich your life, that you like, that could be better, and that you would like changed.

My loved one's behaviors and personal qualities that enrich my life:

_____

My loved one's behaviors and personal qualities that I like:

_____

My loved one's behaviors and personal qualities that could be better:

_____

My loved one's behaviors that I would like changed:

_____

Keep the entire palette in mind when negotiating about any one of the colors.

Power Love Rules for Negotiation

Don't *challenge* your partner or suggest how he or she *should* think or feel; *respectfully* ask for information about his or her perspective.

After you have an understanding of your partner's perspective, give yours, without contradicting your partner.

Focus on the *common* value, what is most important to both of you. For instance, if you're negotiating about a school for your children, acknowledge that you both want what is best for your child and together you want to figure out what that might be. If you don't focus on the common value, a Toddler power struggle is likely to ensue; you'll imply, at least inadvertently, that your partner does not have your child's best interests at heart.

Types of Negotiation

Negotiation styles differ somewhat, depending on which of the three major types of negotiation you attempt: values, temperamental choices, or personal preferences, tastes, and habits.

By far, differences in values represent the greatest test of negotiation skills. Defense of values carries the most intense emotions because values lie at the heart of the sense of self. For example, one partner wants the children exposed to certain religious practices, while the other wants them exposed to different religious traditions or to none at all. The *Power love* negotiation will look something like the following. (Once again, the words you use are not that important. Focus on conveying interest and sincerity, not on word choice):

"I want to understand where you're coming from. Tell me why you feel it's important that the children are not exposed to my religion."

"They'll be confused if they're exposed to two different religions."

"We don't want them confused." (common value). "Let's try to think of ways that exposure to ceremonies from two religions might enrich their experience without confusing them."

In another example, one partner wants to take college courses at night, while the other worries about the expense.

Wrong way:

"We can't afford these courses and you're just selfish for wanting to take them."

"I have a right to take these courses, and you're not going to stop me."

Right way:

"We need opportunities to grow and we want to live within our means, so let's figure out how we can accomplish both goals." (The common values are individual growth and economic security.)

Negotiations that do not apparently tap into conflicts of deeper values include temperamental choices and those that reflect personal preferences and tastes. They usually require behavior requests, specifically, requests for cooperation.

Requesting Cooperation

To achieve a *Power love*, you must accept that in most non-value negotiations, you and your partner are *equally* right. If you accept that your rights are equal, you'll naturally appreciate cooperation rather than demand submission.

Cooperative behavior is intended to achieve a mutual goal. The goal can be specific (clean the room, pay the bill, fold the napkins a certain way), relational (share enriching experience, giving emotional support), or general (achieve closer connection and family harmony).

Step 1: Before you make a behavior request, focus on your deeper values. Ask yourself: "Am I being as compassionate, kind, and loving as I want to be?"

Step 2: Describe the problem and why it's a problem for you. "I get nervous when you're late from work and I don't know if anything's happened to you."

Step 3: Own your vulnerability *and* acknowledge your partner's perspective. "I know my anxiety can be a problem and I *don't* want you to feel controlled."

Step 4: Ask for suggestions to solve the problem. "Is there something we can do so that I don't have to be nervous and you don't have to feel controlled?"

If you suggest a solution, ask if your partner believes it's fair:

"If you're just too busy sometimes, how about if I text you and you just click return or give an ETA (estimated time of arrival), like 7:30, so I know you're all right. Does that sound fair?"

Here's another example: Milly and Jason are applying for a home equity loan. Milly did the research but Jason wants more information.

The Toddler-brain way:

Milly feels insulted, assuming that Jason doesn't trust her to handle the business with the bank. She gives him a patronizing answer about "understanding basic finances." She claims that she can get the loan without his signature, so it doesn't matter what he thinks. Accusing her of trying to hide something, Jason goes to the phone to call the bank loan officer, which causes a review of their previously approved loan.

The Adult-brain way:

"I can tell from your questions that I'm not expressing this well. Let me be sure that you have all the facts so you can feel comfortable signing the loan papers. I want you to sign only if you think it's the best thing for us."

In this response, Milly was the partner she most wanted to be—loving, compassionate, and appreciative of the cooperation she was seeking. She understood that her partner was anxious about the amount. Reassurance and more facts lower anxiety, just as surely as anger and defensiveness raise it. Here is Jason's Adult-brain reply:

"It's not that I don't trust your judgment. I do trust your judgment, I'm just a little nervous about the amount. I know it probably seems like a pain in the neck, but I need some help with more figures."

In this response Jason was the partner he wanted to be—loving, compassionate, and appreciative of the cooperation he was seeking.

In *Power love*, each partner has responsibility to attempt improvement of the interaction, even if the other falters. For example, assume that Milly could not recover from the offense she took at Jason's questions and continued to patronize him. He would maintain respectful, compassionate assertiveness. If Jason lapsed into a Toddler-brain stance of "No! My way," Milly would ask if there is anything she can do now or later to help them arrive at an equitable decision that works for both of them. This is really what love relationships are all about. It's unrealistic to expect that you will both be equally self-regulated at all times. When one can be stronger for the other, the relationship strengthens.

Following the simple steps of negotiation will eliminate no-win Toddler-brain power struggles and get you much more of what you really want: a powerful love that is a close, connected, cooperative relationship.

CHAPTER FIFTEEN

To Get the Partner You Most Want to Have, Be the Partner You Most Want to Be

Your only real chance of getting—and keeping—the partner you most want to have is to be the partner you most want to be. It should be clear by now that you can't be the partner you most want to be until you change Toddler-brain habits. In the Toddler brain, we act on whatever we're feeling at the moment. If the feeling is negative, we're likely to blame it on our partners and behave like the partners we think they *deserve* at that moment, one who is rejecting, resentful, or angry. We saw in Part I how this Toddler-brain response repeated over time will make you lose a sense of who you are and make you act against your nature.

Loss of self is implicit in the dozen or so emails I receive every day from strangers wanting relationship advice. These rather long missives typically focus on complaints about partners. But hidden between the lines is the unspoken query:

"Why do I put up with this?"

And that begs the deeper question: "What kind of person am I?"

And even more important to developing *Power love*: "What kind of partner do I *want* to be?"

To answer these questions adequately, we have to ask four more:

"Do I want to be driven by my ego or motivated by my deepest values?"

"Do I want my partner to submit or to willingly cooperate with me?"

"Do I want to devalue my partner or regard (him or her) as valuable?"

"Which do I want most in my relationship, power or value?"

If you chose the first part of any of the above, you're dragging a chain of resentment through life that keeps you from becoming the person, parent, and intimate partner you most want to be.

Try this experiment. List the personal qualities you would most like to develop. As a guide, think of how you want to be thought of by the people you love and what you might regret the most not doing enough of when you get older. Most of my clients write in this exercise that they want to be more compassionate, kind, appreciative, loving, supportive, and fair and that failing at these is what they would regret most near the end of their lives. Significantly, the latter is consistent with research on late-in-life regret.

Once you come up with your list of qualities you would like to develop, use it to complete the following sentence:

If I were more . . . (for example, compassionate, kind, loving, supportive, appreciative, and fair), *I would* . . . (cite specific behaviors—for example, try hard to understand my partner's perspectives, express support and affection, ensure that I'm being fair, open my heart to beauty in nature, and allow myself to be enhanced by the qualities of people who could enrich my life).

For the next week, do what you wrote above, every day, as often as you can, regardless of what other people do. If you behave consistently according to your deeper values, you will, no doubt, feel more authentic and appreciative at the end of the week. If you do it for six weeks, you'll be well on your way to becoming the partner you most want to be.

The Power to Value

Exerting power is, most of the time, a Toddler-brain opera-tion. In the Adult brain, we create value. Exerting power might sound good, until you ask yourself why you want to do it. In love relationships, if not life in general, people try to exert pow-er when they don't feel *valuable*.

Here's an example from a client. Tammy started the day before her first appointment feeling really down. She woke up that way and was unable to cheer herself out of it. In fact, the feelings worsened as the morning progressed. First her husband injured her sense of entitlement by not cheering her up. (That's right, she felt entitled to be cheered up.) He reacted negatively to her demand that he make her breakfast; eventually he did make her breakfast, albeit with an air of resentment. She didn't notice that her unconscious motivation to avoid the dozens of other pedestrians she passed on her walk to work made her feel worse. Once she got to the office, she wanted her coworkers to be extra nice to her, although she didn't expect that they would be and so wasn't very nice to them.

Some of her coworkers were probably too busy to sense that she felt blue and others, no doubt, reacted negatively to her "attitude"—she thought she overheard one of them say, "Who the hell does she think she is?" Disgusted, she gave up on all of "those insensitive bastards" and went through the entire morning and afternoon in a cold sulk. At the end of the day, she felt that all she needed was a hug and a little sympathy. Predictably, she fell deeper into a depressed mood, perceiving that no one was there for her.

As Tammy described her day in our first session, she sounded very much like the victim of an uncaring environment and an insensitive husband. She thought other people were letting her down, when they were merely reacting to her entitlements and her unfriendliness. Because she felt bad, she devalued her husband as "narcissistic" and "uncaring" and her coworkers as "unreliable" and "just out for themselves" and everyone she passed on the street as "not deserving" regard. The adrenaline rush she got from blaming and devaluing made her feel more powerful for just a little while, before dropping her deeper into depression.

The problem for Tammy—and for the rest of us when we try to substitute power for value—is that we *can't* feel valuable when devaluing someone else, especially loved ones.

Devaluing loved ones is the epitome of a double-edged sword. If part of your deeper values is to respect loved ones, as it is for most people, trying to feel more powerful by devaluing them is the emotional equivalent of trying to quench your thirst by eating sand. When we feel devalued, we have to do something that will make us feel more valuable, not more powerful.

If you're thinking, as I fear some of you are, that you will value other people only if they value you or that you'll be the partner you think your partner deserves, rather than the partner you most want to be, please realize that this sort of Toddler-brain reactivity puts your self-value entirely in the hands of other people. The people who control your self-value are unlikely to react positively to your self-obsession. Locked in the Toddler brain, you'll experience frequent feelings of powerlessness, along with an impulse to feel more powerful by devaluing others. It's the worst kind of downward spiral; the more we try to substitute power for value, the more frequently we'll feel devalued and powerless.

On some level at least, we're aware of the futility of substituting power for value. To take an extreme example, many of the court-ordered batterers I've treated over the years came into their first group session convinced that, as so many of them put it, "If she won't love me, she'll fear me."

Each one of these misguided men knew well that his exertion of power and control over the person he valued most in the world might get him a fearful (and definitely resentful) response but would never inspire the love and respect he wanted. Family abusers feel *unlovable*, which they confuse with feeling powerless. They try to feel more powerful through the adrenaline rush of aggression against their loved ones. I always ask them:

"In the history of humankind, has anyone ever felt more lovable by hurting someone he loves?"

Power Can Never Substitute for Love

I'm quite certain that not many people who read this book fell in love with fantasies of power: "I'm going to make this sucker do whatever I want!"

People fall in love with fantasies of *value*, of loving and being loved. Yet most discord in love relationships rises from

Toddler-brain attempts to substitute power for value. The exertion of power in love sometimes gets compliance (your lover relents and does what you want), sometimes fear, always resentment, but never value. You cannot criticize, stonewall, nag, manipulate, coerce, or threaten someone into genuinely valuing you. More important, you cannot feel valuable while exerting power over loved ones.

The secret of *Power love* lies not in exerting power but in creating value, through interest, compassion, and care.

The self-empowerment that comes from creating value through interest, compassion, and care is its own reward, yet it comes with a significant bonus. The more value we create, the more cooperation and mutuality of giving we are likely to experience in love relationships.

You've probably heard the saying: "Living well is the best revenge." Living well actually means creating more value in your life. Creating more value in your life in general and in your love relationship in particular is the surest way to become the partner you most want to be.

CHAPTER SIXTEEN

Sex and *Power Love*

It should go without saying that love in the Toddler brain pretty much guarantees a bad sex life. When sex happens at all in toddler love, it's dominated by self-obsession, demands, and high emotional reactivity. Putting into practice the suggestions of this book will definitely improve your emotional connection, which is predominantly psychological. But there is also a strong biological element to *Power love*. The bonding hormone oxytocin secreted during orgasm is the largest dose available for men and the second-largest for women. (Breastfeeding provides the biggest dose.) It's much easier to build *Power love* if you have a sex life satisfying to both partners. But to improve your sex life, you can't simply focus on improving your sex life alone. Sexual acts must occur within a general context of intimacy, due to the "85–15 effect."

The figure comes from the research finding that, when both partners report relationship dissatisfaction, 85% cite a bad sex life as a reason for their unhappiness—the sex is too infrequent or unsatisfying or both. But when both partners report high levels of relationship satisfaction, a good sex life accounts for only 15% of it.

You might wonder why sex would have such negative effect when it's bad yet only minor influence when it's good. Well, the answer is on the scoreboard. Yes, the bedroom has a scoreboard—you *know* how many times you have sex.

BEDROOM SCOREBOARD	
Visitors	0
Home	0

Other kinds of intimate behaviors do not have scoreboards. When the relationship is bad, couples are not making eye contact, sharing experiences, offering support, exchanging affection, or enjoying each other's company. They talk *at* each other (not *to* each other) and have a general attitude of disconnection—they see each other as opponents or enemies. But when the relationship is good for both partners, they do make eye contact, share experiences, enjoy each other's company, lend emotional support to each other, talk to each other, frequently express affection, and have a general attitude of connection. In a good relationship, sex is just another good thing; it doesn't stand out as much in a general context of intimacy as it does in an atmosphere of disconnection, in which the "scoreboard" is prominent.

The next chapter shows how to establish a general context of connection. In this one we'll focus on better sex, with the caveat that you must improve other areas of connection as well.

Caution

Many couples fail to improve their sex lives, much less achieve *Power love*, due to a catch-22 that inhibits all manner of behavior change: waiting for feelings to change before you change behavior. Here's how it goes:

"When I feel better I'll exercise." But you're not likely to feel better until you begin regular exercise.

"When I feel less depressed I'll have more interest in life." But you're not likely to feel less depressed until you try hard to take an interest in life.

"We'll start having sex when we feel close and trusting." You're less likely to feel *as* close and trusting as you prefer without having sex, that is, without the oxytocin secreted during sexual intercourse.

Don't feel bad if you're a little confused about sex. The sex lives of modern couples are complex, due to a complicated interplay of *biology*, *psychology*, *culture*, and *relationship dynamics*, in addition to habits of retreating to the Toddler brain under stress.

Biological Changes

We now live longer than any previous generation in the history of *Homo sapiens*. As we age, hormone production diminishes. Worse, we're prone to hormonal imbalances many years before we have a chance to get old. As mentioned in Chapter Six, we've confounded the production and balance of hormones by taking a variety of medications (more than any previous generation) and eating lots of animals overdosed with hormones. What's more, animal studies show that competition for hierarchy greatly affects levels of testosterone. It's reasonable to assume that societal changes in hierarchy and competitiveness do the same for humans.

Testosterone is the major component of sex drives in both men and women. It helps determine not only how frequently men and women want to have sex but how they experience sexual sensation. If a couple fails to appreciate their differences or slips into the Toddler-brain habit of blaming the effects of their hormones on each other, the relationship begins a slow march toward dissolution. Hopefully, a brief description of sex drive differences will help us sympathize with the vulnerabilities they cause.

High-T (testosterone) men and women think a lot about sex. When they fantasize they become sexually aroused; some can have orgasms just through fantasy. They're sexually stimulated by *all* their senses. (A hot bath stimulates more than it soothes.) The heightened pleasure zone tends to be in one place—head of the penis or clitoris. And they can feel physically uncomfortable in prolonged sexual deprivation.

Low-T folks would feel quite comfortable physically if they never had sex. They hardly ever think about it. They're likely to notice the clothing of sexy actors and actresses more than their bodies. Their senses provide aesthetic but not sexual stimulation. (The hot bath calms but doesn't stimulate.) They're unlikely to fantasize about sex, *until* they're aroused—arousal *causes* sexual thoughts. As the renowned sex therapist Pat Love puts it, low-T people don't really desire sex until they're having it. Then, "Wow, I should do this more often!" Areas of heightened pleasure when they are aroused tend to be in several different places in their erogenous zones.

Don't be misled by the likelihood that you and your partner both seemed to be high-T in the early part of your relationship, when nature ramped up your sex drive to unsustainably high levels. There's a Native American saying pertinent to the arc of sex drives in committed relationships:

"If you put a pea in a pot every time you make love in the first year of marriage, and take a pea out every time you make love after that, you'll never empty the pot."

Your true biological sex drive doesn't emerge until near the end of the first year of living together. That's when you need mutual understanding, sympathy, and support.

Of course, T levels are not constant for anyone. They vary with conditions of physical and mental stress, environmental stimulation, degree of competition in the workplaces, and perceived sexual rivals. In everyone, they diminish with age.

The Psychology of Sex

By adulthood everyone has developed unconscious associations with sex and sexual acts. Some are good for intimate connection. For example, many people associate sexual impulse with caring and sensitivity to the inner world of their partners. When that happens, the sensitivity and caring generalizes to their relationship as a whole; if I'm more sensitive in the bedroom, I'm likely to be more sensitive in the kitchen and living room. But many other people have formed associations with sex that produce guilt (it's wrong), shame (I can't do it well), anxiety (something bad will happen), and distaste (it's unclean or disgusting). Still others have learned to view sex as a form of reward or punishment: "You don't deserve it if you don't do what I want!"

The good news about sexual associations is that you can stop reinforcing the bad ones and start creating good ones. This requires willpower and practice more than therapy.

Traditional psychotherapy has proven ineffective with sexual issues when it gets bogged down in trying to figure out why and how your mental associations got started. Besides the fact that we can never know for sure what formed the associations, there's a serious flaw in the therapeutic strategy of "getting to the origin of the problem." Once mental associations become conditioned responses and behavioral habits, it doesn't matter what started them—they run on autopilot, independent of their original cause. For example, consider Pavlov's dogs. The Russian psychologist Ivan Pavlov gained fame in the early twentieth century by conditioning dogs to salivate at the sound of a bell. He simply rang the bell before feeding them. After a few repetitions of getting fed immediately after the ringing of the bell, the dogs got the idea. Of course they didn't think, "Oh, the bell has rung, we are going to be fed!" They reacted automatically, on a visceral level, to the sound of the bell, which their central nervous systems had associated with getting fed. Those dogs continued to salivate at the sound of a bell long after he stopped feeding them. Although feeding them immediately after the bell rang began the conditioned response, the bell, not the feeding, maintained it. If they wanted to change the habit, the researchers would have needed to associate something else with ringing the bell. Conditioned responses and habits can be changed only by forging new ones to replace the old, and that's what we'll do at the end of this chapter.

Passion and Excitement

Excitement is stimulated by the temporary disinhibition of shame or fear. For something to be exciting, there must be a possibility of harm, failure, or exposure to social ridicule or disgust. For instance, it's exciting to take your clothes off in front of your lover only because it's shameful to do it in the hotel lobby. It's not exciting for nudists to undress in front of each other.

The excitement that sex holds for humans goes far beyond the brief arousal–climax cycle we share with all mammals. Unlike other animals, humans have traditionally heaped mounds of shame onto sexual expression, which makes it all the more exciting. The rapture of sexual excitement owes to the feeling of acceptance and success in the face of possible rejection or failure. As the subtle backdrop of rejection or failure declines, as it must in intimate relationships that go well beyond one-night stands, the excitement of sex diminishes. At that point the passion of intimacy (emotional connection with the unique person you love) must compensate for the loss of excitement in overcoming the threat of rejection or failure.

The possibility of shame (or harm) necessary for excitement is by no means limited to sex. The emotional rush we get from successful performance of any kind depends entirely on the possibility of failure. Tasks done with ease, with no possibility of failure, are boring. The thrill of athletic contests rises and falls with the possibility of losing. The favored team winning by a lot is run-of-the-mill and hardly an interesting contest. But if the game is close, with the heavily favored team in danger of losing, it becomes exciting. Excitement attaches to winning only when it must overcome formidable barriers, such as a major upset or a come-from-behind drive for the winning score.

The prospect of overcoming shame-based inhibition is an important component of attraction. There is little excitement in an attraction when we know for certain that we won't be rejected. Unfortunately, this also provides the excitement of unwise or forbidden attractions, such as affairs, certain kinds of pornography, incest, and the "rescuing" behaviors that begin many hapless unions—"saving" the alcoholic, the hurt and lonely, the depressed and anxious, the victim, the loser, the abuser, or the criminal.

Failure to inhibit shame can make us isolate or form attachments based on a false self—a phony one we hope will not be rejected. It can also create a disgust reaction to certain normal sexual behavior: "Only an animal would do something like that!" What used to be called "sexual hang-ups" are really failures to disinhibit shame.

Other sexual problems can result from too easily disinhibiting shame, leading to premature orgasm or excitement that dissipates in foreplay, once the aroused state feels like the norm. Those are the people who want foreplay to be short and not necessarily sweet.

Sex and Culture

Most cultures and religions have traditionally surrounded sex with a lot of guilt and shame, mostly to stabilize marriage and families. At the same time, modern Western cultures offer a constant barrage of sexual imagery and stimulation through ubiquitous media. (Media designers quite literally "pimp" their advertisers' products these days.) The constancy of sexual images, coupled with cultural and religious dogma about sex, form a continual stimulation-shame-excitement cycle. Sex within a committed relationship, by comparison, is less exciting.

Ironically, the cultural and religious inhibitions about sex designed to stabilize families now have opposite effects. The people who most internalize culturally inspired or religiously induced guilt and shame over sex are more likely to have extramarital affairs, "seduced" by the excitement of overcoming their formidable inhibitions.

In *Power love*, couples establish their own standards concerning sex. They decide together what will bring them closer, while remaining true to their most humane values.

Sex and Relationship Dynamics

The typical relationship dynamic around sex is a power struggle over whose sexual preferences (or lack of them) will dominate. The high-T partner is likely to cajole or coerce more sex, which the low-T partner resists and vetoes. The high-T partner feels rejected and isolated; the low-T partner feels pressured, objectified, and used. Both are apt to pathologize the other's sex drive:

"You're frigid!"

"You're an animal! A sex addict!"

In reality, it's the relationship dynamic of power struggles that's pathological, not sex drives. Both high and low T levels are perfectly normal!

Disparate sex drives require understanding, sympathy, and teamwork. That cannot happen when partners pathologize or blame each other or turn the beloved into an opponent.

Power Love Sex

As with any problem important to your future and your family's welfare, you want your solutions to come from your deeper values rather than temporary feelings. Decide what kind of relationship you want to have and let your deeper values guide you toward it.

Because different sex drives make it hard to feel empathy for each other (you can't really get what it's like for your partner), you must develop a higher level of compassion. When in touch with your most humane values, neither of you wants the other to be uncomfortable, rejected, or pressured. With that common value as your starting point, the mutual caring that follows will bring you closer together. In your Adult brains, you each want your partner to feel valued, loved, and desired, just as much as you want those things for yourself. In your Adult brains, you both want to give and receive pleasure and sexual satisfaction.

The low-T partner has the greatest leverage in moving the couple toward a satisfying sex life. The high-T partner is limited to compassion and understanding, no small thing to be sure, but also no guarantee that it will increase your partner's sex drive. If you're a low-T person, develop your own sexuality instead of reacting to your partner's.

Take charge of your sexuality. Appreciate that you are a sexual being. That biological fact runs deeper than any psychological, cultural, or relationship issue. Think of when you've enjoyed sex in the past; imagine those times in detail, particularly what you were doing and feeling. Set aside a few minutes each day to think about sex. Experiment with your body to find what most appeals to you. This is the only life you get. Do you really want it to be sexually deprived?

Of course, establishing the general context of intimacy required of *Power love* is never just one partner's task. And it's never a matter of getting one partner to do something. The crucial thing to remember is to replace Toddler-brain blame, denial, and avoidance with Adult-brain improve, appreciate, connect, and protect. The question is always:

"What can *we* do to feel closer and experience pleasure together?"

Creating Positive Mental Associations about Sex

If the frequency or quality of sex in your relationship is an issue, it's a pretty safe bet that one or both of you have made some negative mental associations with sexual acts. You can use the **TIP** process to correct those in the following way.

List any negative mental associations you might have about sex (example: pressure, boring, painful, dark, sad):

_____

_____

_____

List the mental associations about sex you would like to develop (example: warm, passionate, transcendent):

_____

_____

_____

TIP

Think repeatedly about your positive associations. If you journal, write about them (for example, "Sex with my partner is . . . warm, passionate, transcendent.")
Imagine in detail the sex you would like to have.
Practice the new mental associations in your partner's presence.

Set aside two to three minutes for each practice session. After each practice session, make a mental note of how much more valuable the new associations make you feel, compared to the old response of resentment or disappointment.

Daily Log (with number of times practiced)

Negative Associations	New Associations

CHAPTER SEVENTEEN

Empowering *Power Love*

Falling in love is as natural as death. Staying in love is as natural as good diet and healthy exercise. Just about everyone can eat, exercise, and love well in the short run. But over the long haul of everyday modern living, we shoot ourselves in the foot, simply because we try to do these life-sustaining activities in the wrong part of the brain, that is, the Toddler brain. Since this chapter is not about how we shoot ourselves in the foot concerning diet and exercise, I'll just say that maintaining love relationships requires dedication and discipline approaching that of exercise and healthy eating.

We primarily shoot ourselves in the foot in love by acting on feelings. Acting on feelings got you into a love relationship and is sure to get you out of it. The initial burst of hormones that produce the intense feelings of love lasts only for a few months. Fidelity to deeper values sustains love for the long haul. The power of love comes not from what it feels like but from the value, meaning, and purpose it adds to living.

Love relationships are difficult to maintain in large part because our culture continues to elevate Toddler-brain feelings above values. People feel entitled to express every negative feeling they have, without regard to the effects on others, just as they felt entitled to litter a few decades ago and to smoke in public buildings a few years ago. Some pop-psychology books even claim that to be "real," we have to explore and express *all* feelings—none is too small for exploration and expression.

Besides the fact that "exploring" and expressing feelings amplifies and magnifies, that is, *distorts* them, the self-obsessed exploration process makes it difficult to see our partners (or anyone else) as complex individuals, distinct from our current feelings about them. In effect, exploring and expressing feelings keeps us trapped in the Toddler brain.

To feel genuine and empowered in love relationships, we need to know more than whether our feelings are valid or justified. We need to know how they help or hinder us as intimate partners. No matter how valid and "appropriate" Toddler-brain feelings of entitlement, resentment, or anger may seem, the more important questions, once again, are these:

"Is my entitlement, resentment, or anger reflecting the kind of person and partner I most want to be?"

"Am I blaming my failure to be the person and partner I most want to be on someone else?"

Attitude of Connection

You've probably tried lots of things to improve your relationship. If what you've tried has failed, it was likely due to an attitude of disconnection forged by Toddler-brain habits. When the default attitude is disconnection, blame, denial, and avoidance dominate the relationship. With an attitude of disconnection, all attempts to negotiate turn into coercion, due to the overwhelming subtext:

"I can't connect with you until you do what I want."

In Toddler-brain love, every disagreement causes emotional divorce. With an *attitude of connection*, specific behaviors are negotiable but not the connection:

"We need to . . ." (for example, respect each other) to enhance the connection we both value."

I once saw a research recording of interviews with couples in long-term happy marriages. One particular couple was married for 60 years. They asked the wife if, in all those years, she ever thought about divorce. She replied immediately and incredulously:

"*Divorce?* Never!" After a moment, she shrugged and said with a tiny smile, "Murder maybe, but never divorce."

Aside from the sheer humor of her response (and she wasn't trying to be funny), she made a point that clearly distinguishes long-term happy relationships from terrible ones. When you live together, your partner will occasionally do things that irritate you and you might get pretty angry. But you always know that the negative feeling will pass and what really matters is the connection.

I've written about an attitude of connection in other books and articles, but it would be remiss of me not to repeat it in a book on *Power love*. Developing an attitude of connection requires *mindful effort* in the beginning, if Toddler-brain coping mechanisms have formed entrenched habits. But the more you practice connective thoughts and behaviors, the easier and more natural it becomes.

Couples with an attitude of connection (that is, happy couples) regard themselves as connected, behave as if they're connected, root their connection in common values, build lifelines, maintain goodwill, engage in a spirit of cooperation, try to be flexible, seek to understand each other, and establish brief but frequent routine rituals of connection. We'll address each of these Adult-brain qualities below.

Regard Yourself As Connected

An easy way to regard yourself as connected is to make a simple semantic shift. Research shows that unhappy couples (with an attitude of disconnection) think and speak in terms of "Me," "I," "You," "Mine," "Yours." In contrast, happy partners (with an attitude of connection) think and speak with the plural pronouns: "We," "Us," "Our." Working "we, us, ours" into your everyday vocabulary strengthens your attitude of connection. Try writing this sentence a couple of times to see how it feels to you:

"*We* want *our* relationship to bring *us* the safety, security, love, and happiness *we* both want and deserve."

Behave As If You're Connected

Avoid the trap of waiting until you feel closer to behave in loving ways. When you behave as if you are connected, you're likely to think in terms of couple-hood and, eventually, feel more connected.

The following exercises can help to nurture an attitude of connection.

Connection Exercises:

List what you would do differently if you felt more connected to your partner. (Example: touch more, make more eye contact, embrace more, go for walks together, that is, share experiences.)

1. _____

2. _____

3. _____

4. _____

5. _____

Describe three things you would do first thing in the morning, if you woke up tomorrow *happily married* and *totally satisfied* with your relationship:

1. _____

2. _____

3. _____

As an experiment for the next month, practice every day what you wrote in the above exercises. Don't wait until you feel like doing it. Practice the behavior and the feelings will follow.

Root Your Connection in Common Values

Deep connection is not based on shared preferences of what you like and enjoy. Rather, it's based on shared values. Common interests often attract people, but common values sustain relationships. A couple whose connection is based on common interests without common values will likely become competitive in their interests; partners will try to hike farther or faster than the other. Attuned to their deeper values, they'll place more importance on sharing the experience of hiking in each other's company.

Values Connection

List areas of deep connection (based on values) that you might possibly develop in the future. (Try to think in terms of mutual activities, for example, joining community groups, sharing spiritual experiences, nature trips, art trips, and so on.)

1. _____

2. _____

3. _____

Build Lifelines

Like the lines that astronauts use to keep attached to their space vehicles, emotional lifelines provide maximum movement, while providing life-saving connection. As a relationship metaphor, lifelines keep us anchored to what matters most.

Imagine a long, flexible lifeline that constantly connects you and your partner. No matter what you're doing or feeling, you remain connected. Even when angry at each other, or when you need a time-out to get away from each other, you're still connected. If you imagine a constant connection by an invisible lifeline, your unconscious emotional demeanor around your partner will change for the better, increasing the likelihood of positive response from your partner. Bad moments will occur less frequently and will be shorter-lived, because they won't trigger disconnection.

My Lifeline to You

Maintain goodwill. Stay focused on what is best for both of you. You both want to be well, with neither of you feeling put down, taken advantage of, devalued, or disregarded. Appreciate how your partner enriches your life and that will encourage your partner to do the same.

Engage in a spirit of cooperation. Work together as a team for the best interests of your family. Remember always that the valued self cooperates and the devalued self resists. Give the value you want to receive.

Try to be flexible. Life is cruel to the rigid but generally kind to the flexible. Be as flexible as you can while respecting your deeper values, and you'll be happier and love better.

Seek to understand each other. Rather than argue, try to understand each other's perspectives. Instead of refuting or contradicting your partner, seek and add more information.

Establish brief but frequent routine rituals of connection. I developed the *Power Love Formula* more than fifteen years ago. It's been a huge predictor of success in our boot camps for highly distressed couples, either already separated or on the verge of separation. Couples who do it faithfully have vastly improved relationships a year later. The *Power Love Formula* incorporates small moments of connection into your daily routine.

The principle of small moments of connection has more empirical support in the work of Barbara Fredrickson at the University of North Carolina. Her research shows that what she calls "micro moments of love" improve individual health and well-being as well as relationships.

Small gestures of connection built into your daily routine do wonders to create a stable attitude of connection. In contrast, special events, like romantic weekends or nice vacations, while they may be pleasant or enjoyable, are often followed by a letdown when the unsustainable wave of well-being crashes back to the routine of daily living. Don't get me wrong—romantic weekends, nice vacations, and the like are good for relationships, *if* there is also routine connection. The safety and security that will help you repair your relationship rises from a steady attitude of connection rather than big waves of emotional experience. The secret to loving big is thinking small.

I have found that change in my clients' behavior becomes permanent when connective behaviors are small enough to fit into a daily routine. To that end, I designed the *Power Love Formula,* which takes less than five minutes a day. Each iteration should begin with a conscious awareness of why you are doing it—*to strengthen your connection.*

Here are the four steps of the *Power Love Formula:*

Step 1: Importance gesture

Make some gesture of your partner's importance to you at four crucial times of the day. As a general rule, any behaviors we do during transitional times have more carryover effect, as we're more likely to take current attitudes into the next circumstance we encounter. One of the best behaviors you can do for your personal health and the well-being of your relationship is affirm your partner's importance to you first thing in the morning. Your second daily acknowledgement, just before you leave the house in the morning, creates a positive image of your partner to carry with you while you're apart. The third sets a positive tone for spending the pre-bedtime hours together. Your final daily acknowledgment will sweeten your dreams and carry your love into the next morning.

Your *importance gesture* is a way of keeping your partner close to your heart. Come up with a brief, nonverbal gesture that acknowledges your partner's significance to you. (We have to pay more attention to nonverbal gestures; words can be said by rote.) It can be a touch, gentle eye contact, or simply reaching out your hand. Only the two of you need know what the gesture means. It can be your precious secret.

Step 2: Hug 6 x 6

Hugs are usually the first thing to go once a relationship is ruled by Toddler-brain blame, denial, and avoidance. Over time, failure to embrace becomes a prescription for disaster; the less you touch, the more resentful you get, and the more resentful you get, the less you touch. The following routine, which takes 36 seconds per day, is designed to reverse this downward momentum.

Hug your partner, in a full-body embrace—with as many of your body parts touching as possible—a minimum of six times a day, holding each hug for a minimum of six seconds. (Full-body embrace is one of the few reliable ways that men get oxytocin—the bonding hormone that makes us feel close, connected, calm, and trusting.) The 6 x 6 formula is not arbitrary. You probably do not hug more than once or twice a day now. Increasing that to six times per day will facilitate a new level of closeness. The six-second minimum for each hug recognizes the fact that in the beginning, many of those hugs will be forced. Even if they start out forced, they are likely to become genuine at about the fourth or fifth second, provided you're still attached to each other. This kind of embrace also increases serotonin levels that help reduce appetite. Not a bad deal—you'll feel better, with less edginess, irritability, and sadness, and just maybe you'll drop a pound or two in the process of feeling closer.

Step 3: Indulge in positive thoughts about your relationship

This is easy. At some point during your workday, stop for 10 seconds to think positive thoughts about your partner. List a few below:

1. _____

2. _____

3. _____

4. _____

5. _____

Step 4: The love contract

Write the following out as a formal contract. Keep it brief and simple. Do it at an agreed-upon time every day. It is a symbolic expression of your love. *I hereby agree to show my love for you every day by* (doing *one* of the following):

1. Lighting a candle for you

2. Posting an "I love you" note

3. Putting a flower petal on your breakfast plate

4. Sending an "I love you" text message

5. Writing one line of our favorite song

6. Other _____

The simple, daily behaviors of the *Power Love Formula* will help revitalize your emotional connection. But the good it will do is not accomplished in any one or several implementations. The overall benefit of the *Power Love Formula* lies in the accumulative effect of a steady connection over time.

Caveat: Once you start the *Power Love Formula*, you must continue it for at least a year. View it as a relationship commitment. There are two compelling reasons for maintaining the commitment.

The *Power Love Formula* is more powerful during distant or conflict periods of a relationship than at close times, proving that even when things aren't great, your connection remains important. However, it will have a negative effect if you stop it because you're mad at your partner or because you get bored with it. Then the message is that your relationship (and your partner) is not worth five minutes a day. Stay with the commitment and, over time, you'll reap the reward of a closer, more emotionally connected relationship.

Power Love Values

To begin building a powerful relationship of adult love, try an experiment for at least a month. Put whatever you're feeling on the back burner and dedicate all your efforts to strengthening the *Power love* values listed below. Each one is supported by research on characteristics of long-term happy relationships. If you and your partner make a sincere effort to enhance all of them, you will find, after a month or so, that you *feel* considerably more love for each other.

The power love values are:

Equality: Rights, preferences, and responsibilities are more or less equal; neither partner has authority over the other.

Fairness: Partners maintain mutually acceptable division of labor and responsibility for the maintenance, growth, and well-being of the family.

Friendship/support: Partners confide in each other, without fear of judgment or criticism, and are "there" for each other.

Loving behavior: Partners are compassionate and kind, showing care and desire to help when one is distressed, hurt, or in need of help. They engage in mutually satisfying physical affection, sexual passion, and meaningful or enjoyable activities.

Playfulness: Partners enjoy each other's company and sharing certain experiences. They like to have fun together.

To Love Well, You Have to Sometimes Feel Inadequate

If *Power love* values seem like new territory for you, just thinking about them is likely to stir feelings of inadequacy, which in turn breed irritability or resentment. Ignore the irritability and resentment—those are just smoke. The fire is a perception of inadequacy, however temporary it might be. In the Adult brain, feelings of inadequacy are seen as important motivators; it would hardly be possible to have a *Power love* without the occasional experience of inadequacy. A stab of inadequacy motivates us to do something that makes us feel more adequate. If you have children, the inadequacy you felt when you first heard your infant give out an intensely distressed cry (that unmistakable and unbearable "Wahhh!!!") was a powerful motivation to help. Helping the child was the only way to feel adequate at that moment. If you had suppressed or tried to avoid that uncomfortable feeling or, worse, blamed it on the distressed child, you would not have felt the same urge to provide effective care. Studies of primates show that the typically hysterical response of mothers when forcibly separated from their infants is completely eliminated after shots of morphine. With their feelings of inadequacy numbed by drugs, addicted human mothers are likely to neglect or abandon their newborns. But once they're sober and the sense of inadequacy is allowed to motivate caregiving, they once again nurture their children or try to recover rights to those they lost during their addiction.

Everything significant that you have learned in your life stimulated at least a brief feeling of inadequacy when you first attempted it. Think of the struggle of learning a new skill or a sport or starting a new job. The uncomfortable feeling of inadequacy motivated you to learn how to do the job or acquire the skill. You have many times replaced the terrible feeling of inadequacy with the pleasant feeling of competence. You can do the same with love.

In summary, we can empower love relationships with a few adjustments to daily routine. The first is assuming an attitude of connection, which means regarding ourselves as connected and behaving as if we're connected, even when we don't feel like it. Over time, an attitude of connection changes negative feelings to positive, while an attitude of disconnection guarantees that negative feelings will come to dominate the relationship. The *Power Love Formula* takes less than five minutes a day and, done every day, is almost certain to reinforce attitudes of connection. Relationships are stronger when we keep focused on common values, rather than temporary feelings. Adherence to the *Power love* values of equality, fairness, friendship/support, loving behavior, and playfulness greatly strengthens relationships. Feelings of inadequacy about love relationships are not signals of failure but motivations to be true to the *Power love* values.

Now we are ready to learn how to love our partners and to teach them how to love us.

CHAPTER EIGHTEEN

The Most Loving Thing You Can Say to Your Partner: *Teach Me How to Love You*

There's one more way the Toddler brain can undermine our best attempts to build a powerful relationship. It might be the hardest to detect, because it's often dressed in the cloak of compassion, kindness, and love.

In the Toddler brain, we're likely to give our partners the support, help, affection, and love we *want to give*, rather than what they *want to receive*, like the toddler who offers you candy when you're hungry for sirloin. It's easiest to see this hidden influence of the Toddler brain in regard to core vulnerabilities. The support I want from my partner when I'm trying to avoid shame is in the form of joint activity, like hiking, going to a concert or an art gallery, or talking about anything, *except* what might have stimulated the shame, at least until I feel ready to solve whatever it was. So my instinct when she's anxious or fearful is to offer these things to her, and in the Toddler brain, I would feel rejected or resentful when she responded negatively to my offerings.

But in my Adult brain, I appreciate that none of the things I would wish for when I'm trying to avoid shame would help her anxiety. Rather, she wants us to talk specifically about what stimulates the anxiety, while I show that she is not alone in her concerns and that I care about her. A similar divide between what one partner wants to give and the other prefers to receive can exist in any act of compassion, kindness, and love.

Freedom to Learn

One of the worst things we can do for the health of our relationships is pretend that we know how to make intimate unions work. That Toddler-brain illusion keeps us from learning how to love our partners. Instead, we'll conclude that they're unable or unwilling to do what we "know" would make our relationships succeed. In reality, there's no way that any of us *could* know how to make modern intimate relationships work. Biology has not prepared us for love's special challenges in our rapidly changing culture. Tradition is hopelessly outdated—the old socialized roles and norms have broken down almost completely. And pop psychology gives little more than platitudes or oversimplified and contradictory advice or "communication techniques" that are so unnatural, you'll just end up resenting each other for failing to do them consistently.

However, the Adult brain is amazingly adaptive and eminently capable of learning. The *only* thing that blocks us from learning how to maintain loving relationships with the people we love is the ego; we simply don't want to admit that we don't know how to do it.

Let's here and now relieve ourselves of the awful burden of having to defend an ego that's unrealistically inflated when it comes to love relationships. Repeat the following out loud, at least three times, or until you feel a sense of relief:

"I don't know what the hell I'm doing when it comes to making a modern intimate relationship work!"

Now that you no longer have to defend egotistical preconceptions of how relationships *should* be, you're free to apply Adult-brain power to learning *how* to love the unique person with whom you want to share your life. The most loving thing you can say to your partner is:

"Teach me how to love you, and I will teach you how to love me."

Make It Easy for Your Partner to Love You

In the Toddler brain, we make it hard for our partners to love us, through chronic blame, denial, and avoidance. The objective of *Power love* is just the opposite—to make it easy. The best way to accomplish this—and it's not rocket science—is to love them the way they want to be loved, thereby increasing the likelihood of heartfelt reciprocation. The following will definitely help.

Ask your partner: *What can I do to make you feel loved?* Write down your partner's response (example: "Surprise me now and then with flowers").

Assuming that your partner responds with something you can do, say: *This will make it easier for me to do what will make you feel loved* (example: "Show me that you're pleased with the flowers when I bring them").

Compile a list of things your partner would like you to do to make him or her feel loved, along with what your partner can do to make it easier for you to do those things.

1. _____

2. _____

3. _____

4. _____

5. _____

Tell your partner: *I feel loved when you* (example: "greet me when I come home").

How can I make it easier for you to do this? Write your partner's response (example: "Showing appreciation when you do it and doing the same for you").

Compile a list of things you would like your partner to do to make you feel loved and what you can do to make it easier for him or her to do those things.

1. _____

2. _____

3. _____

4. _____

5. _____

If your relationship has been dominated by Toddler-brain blame, denial, or avoidance, the level of automatic reactivity between you won't disappear overnight. Until you develop Adult-brain habits (which takes about six weeks of practice), you'll need to try consciously to resist the chain reaction of blame, denial, and avoidance when one of you slips into an old habit.

Your best chance of getting the relationship you both want is for *each* of you to commit to change *unilaterally*, regardless of whether you feel that your partner is changing. This will give you both room to recover from lapses while developing new habits. More important, it will help each of you be the person and partner you most want to be.

For the next six weeks, forego the impulse to punish your partner for the inevitable behavioral slips. Keep score only of your own success in doing your part, not of your partner's failure to do his or her part.

Stand up and read the following resolution out loud. Remember, we tend to be more committed to declarations we make out loud while standing.

"For the next six weeks, I will unconditionally:

"Make an effort to see you and hear you. (For example, "I'll fight my habit of mind-wandering when you talk.")

"Make an effort to help you be well. (For example, help you as much as I can and try to take pressure off you.)

"Appreciate your contributions to my life.

"Regard your desires and preferences as equal to mine.

"Create reasons to be happy.

"Make behavior requests from my core value, that is, respectfully, without devaluing you.

"Acknowledge your efforts to improve.

"Try hard to recover and repair as quickly as I am able if I slip into Toddler-brain habits.

"Try to maintain compassion and kindness when you slip into Toddler-brain habits.

"Try to feel closer and more connected.

"Try to feel sexier."

Golden Promise: If you consistently do the above for 30 days, you'll likely achieve a *Power love.*

Epilogue and Summary

P *ower love* transcends the limits of emotional habits and allows us to become the most empowered and humane partners we can be. In *Power love* we build relationships based on desire rather than emotional need, on support rather than demands, on enduring values rather than temporary feelings.

To achieve a *Power love*:

- Balance your competing drives for autonomy and connection.

- Observe the Laws of Emotional Bonds.

- Hold onto self-value and value for your partner when you disagree.

- Work as a team to deactivate your intimate relationship dynamics.

- Practice binocular vision.

- Respect individuality and honor differences.

- Become the partner you most want to be.

- Soar with sexual intimacy.

- Build habits of connection.

- Let your partner teach you how to love him or her.

- Teach your partner how to love you.

Balance your competing drives for autonomy and connection by acting on your deepest values. Acting consistently on your deepest, most humane values makes you feel authentically adult. Value-driven behavior keeps you focused on what is most important to and about you. The fuel of *Power love* is fidelity to our deepest, most humane values of compassion, kindness, protection, and affection. When true to our deeper values, we automatically balance the opposing drives for autonomy and connection. We feel at once more authentic and true to ourselves while investing in the well-being of those we love. We recognize that we cannot be happy in an intimate relationship without being compassionate and kind.

Observe the Laws of Emotional Bonds. Emotional signals in intimate relationships, particularly guilt and shame, are really distance regulators. When we act on them to get closer, they ameliorate. When we don't, they worsen.

Hold onto self-value and value for your partner when you disagree. Adults in love hold onto self-value when they don't like each other's behavior, so they don't feel devalued by the behavior. This enables them to hold onto value for their partners, so they don't devalue them under stress. Rather than helplessly reacting like toddlers, they tap into their deeper value of supporting each other's well-being, even when they disagree or when they feel bad.

Work as a team to deactivate your intimate relationship dynamics. *Power Love* transcends all stress-induced habits that activate Toddler-brain coping mechanisms, which are the fuel of intimate relationship dynamics. These dynamics cannot be overcome by blaming them on your partner. Rather, you must work together to identify the dynamic and deactivate it, by declaring that your connection is more important than the dynamic. When you're connected, you can solve problems. When you're disconnected, the problems are bigger than you.

Practice binocular vision. The reality of your relationship is two perspectives together. Never make a judgment about a specific interaction—or about your relationship in general— without understanding your partner's perspective. When in doubt, get more information about your partner's perspective before giving more about yours.

Respect individuality and honor differences. Accept that you are different from your partner in a great many dimensions and that you almost certainly give different emotional meanings to common events and experiences. The secret of happy relationships is to appreciate as many differences as you can and tolerate the ones you can't appreciate. Disagreements can actually enrich relationships by adding depth and dynamism.

Become the partner you most want to be. Your only chance of getting the partner you most want to have is to be the partner you most want to be. In the Toddler brain, reactive partners are stuck on a treadmill of behaving like the partners they think their partners deserve. Only in the Adult brain can you heal, grow, and thrive by staying true to your deepest, most humane values.

Soar with sexual intimacy. When in touch with our most humane values, the Adult brain is fully activated; we want our partners to feel valued, loved, and desired. We want to give and receive pleasure and sexual satisfaction. The passion of *Power love* goes well beyond mere excitement to achieve a deep emotional connection with the unique person you love.

Build habits of connection. Intimate connection is largely a matter of attitude and habit. We choose to regard ourselves as connected and we choose to feel disconnected. In general, you'll like yourself more when you choose connection and less when you choose disconnection. To love like empowered adults, build habits of brief moments of connection and structure them into your daily routine.

Let your partner teach you how to love him or her and teach your partner how to love you. Love looks a little different for each person. Discover what makes you feel loved and what makes your partner feel loved. Your mutual desire to support each other will make your love soar.

The Road to *Power Love*

The road to *Power love* begins with self-regulation, which is the only way to override Toddler-brain habits. It requires a journey based on our deepest, most humane values and commitment to create a relationship of equality and partnership, which, above all, nurtures mutual growth, respect, and affection.

APPENDIX

The Toddler Love Epidemic

Almost all my clients in the past fifteen years or so have come to me by way of referrals from other therapists. Many previous therapists have given up, not on my clients as individuals, but on their struggles to maintain committed relationships. They see me as a last resort before the dissolution of the relationship.

I deeply believe that most of these unhappy couples have been victimized by a terrible trend in the culture of pop psychology and, to a lesser extent, in a particular school of couples' counseling and therapy. This troubling trend has the effect of promoting Toddler-brain love, through the declaration, based on little or no empirical evidence, that adults have "emotional needs," which must be mirrored and validated by their intimate partners.

Now that you know how to build a powerful, enduring love in the Adult brain, you'll be able to recognize how certain concepts and techniques tragically keep so many people trapped in Toddler-brain relationships.

The Curse of "Emotional Needs"

The notion of emotional needs is one of the more harmful contributions of the pop-psychology culture, at least for those who buy into the concept, and for those who live with someone who buys into it. The term came into popular parlance during the 1980s. For some sociologists, that was the beginning of the era of self-obsession, which has grown steadily, as scores on measures of narcissism have indicated ever since.

The idea of emotional needs is derived from a misunderstanding of Abraham Maslow's theory of motivation known as the "Hierarchy of Needs." (I think today he would call it "Hierarchy of Motivation," given how the term "emotional needs" has been abused in pop psychology.) First published in 1943, Maslow's original hierarchy begins with the most fundamental of motivations (eating, sleeping, excreting, and so on) and culminates with self-actualization—growing to achieve one's fullest potential. Maslow later criticized his own concept of self-actualization, adding a new top layer to the hierarchy, which he called self-transcendence. He argued in this new version that we only find actualization by giving ourselves to some higher goal outside the self, in altruism and spirituality. His concept of transcendence echoes the call from ancient religious and spiritual sources to "find yourself by losing yourself."

It's important to note that Maslow's Hierarchy was largely part of a developmental theory, that is, a description of the differential importance of various motivations as children develop into adults and adults grow to their fullest potential— or, in the vocabulary of this book, how toddlers grow into adults who can use the profoundest part of their brains under stress to achieve fidelity to their deepest values.

There is no question that young children have emotional needs in the development of a stable and cohesive sense of self and that they need help from adults to develop that sense of self. It's also true that toddlers cannot distinguish wanting something from needing it, which is why they can get so hurt or tantrum-prone when we say no to something they want but obviously do not need, like a toy or a treat. At the moment they want it, it *feels* like they need it; the stronger the feeling, the more it seems that they *need* it. The Toddler brain's misinterpretation of strong feelings in relationships is how we confuse wanting, preferring, and desiring with needing. It's how we create the sense that a lover (parent-figure) must mirror and validate our feelings so we can have a cohesive sense of self.

There's a biological explanation of why adults, with a powerful prefrontal cortex, continue to conflate wanting, preferring, and desiring with *need*. The perception of need begins with a rise in emotional intensity. As the intensity increases, it can feel like you need to do or have something, for one reason: It's the *same emotional process as biological need*. (You can observe the process by planting your face in a pillow—emotional intensity rises just before you struggle to breathe, or by delaying urination—emotional intensity rises before there is pain in the bladder.) When emotion suddenly rises, your brain confuses preferences with biological needs. In other words, the perception of need becomes self-reinforcing: "I feel it, therefore I need it; and if I need it, I have to feel it more intensely."

The perception of need falsely explains much of our negative experience in intimate relationships. If I feel bad in any way for any reason, it's because my partner isn't meeting my needs. It doesn't matter that I'm tired, not exercising, bored, ineffective at work, or stressed from the commute and the declining stock market, or if I'm mistreating you or otherwise violating my values; I'm convinced that I feel bad because you're not meeting my needs.

The perception of emotional needs justifies and inflames Toddler-brain entitlement: "I have a right to get you to do what I want, because I *need* it, and my right is superior to your right not to do it."

And let's not forget the coercive element of emotional need: "If you don't do what I need, you'll be punished in some way," at least by withdrawal of affection.

Once the mind becomes convinced that it needs something, pursuit of it can easily become obsessive, compulsive, or addictive. Obsessing about the object of "need" increases emotional intensity and the perception of need—the more I think about what you should do for me, the stronger the perceived need grows.

In terms of motivation, emotional needs are similar to maintenance addictions, those that cause discomfort in withdrawal, with no stimulation of reward centers in the brain when gratified. Over time, there's little or no reward in "getting my needs met" and lots of resentment when they are not. I may not even notice when you do what I want, but I'll be angry or depressed when you don't.

No matter how seductive "I need you" may sound in popular songs, the partner who needs you cannot freely love you. In fact, if someone needs you, he or she is more likely to abuse you than to give freely of love and support. Most painful conflicts in Toddler-brain relationships begin with one partner making an emotional demand, motivated by a perceived "need," that the other, motivated by a different "need," regards as unfair. This conflict is practically inevitable as the Grand Human Contradiction makes us struggle to balance autonomy and connection. The result is the classic Toddler-brain standoff:

"If you loved me, you would agree with me and do what I want."

"If you loved *me*, you would agree with me, and not ask me to do what you want."

"Mine!"

"No!"

Any disagreement can feel like a threat through the lens of perceived "need." When we "need" someone to agree with us or do what we want, we're likely to be controlling, demanding, manipulative, coercive, even abusive.

In contrast to feelings of entitlement that go with the perception of emotional needs, preferring or desiring the people we love to do what we want will likely make us more agreeable, respectful, and cooperative. Wanting is more likely than demanding to get us what we want.

Toddlers Have Emotional Needs

The primary emotional needs of toddlers, in addition to safety, security, and love, are *validation, mirroring,* and *self-regulation modeling.* Mirroring is reflecting back the experience of the child: "I see that you feel bad, and I'm so sorry. I feel bad that you feel bad." Validation is understanding and expressing acceptance of the child's experience: "It's understandable and it's okay that you feel bad." Self-regulation modeling (cheering yourself up when down and calming yourself when upset) is showing the child how to achieve equilibrium: "I'm sorry you feel bad; let's see what we can do to help." Mirroring, validation, and self-regulation help young children develop confidence in their perceptions of the world and, eventually, their ability to cope with it. Remember, the Toddler brain has no reality testing; toddlers *need* adults to help them develop a sense of reality that is independent of, but compatible with, their feelings about it.

Validation vs. Empowerment

Emotional validation is understanding and expressing acceptance of another person's emotional experience. Young children certainly need to have their experience validated by their parents, as the emerging sense of self is fragile and unable to reconcile thoughts and feelings with what is happening around them. But in most interactions between adults, validation is more complicated than that which toddlers need from their parents. In adult interactions, validation must be mutual and respectful of differences in perspective.

In my long practice, I have never seen an adult who was resentful about not feeling "validated" who was in the least interested in validating anyone's experience that differed from his or her own. In fact, adults in the Toddler brain are more likely to *invalidate*—reject, ignore, or judge—other people's experience when they decide that it differs from their own.

Emotional validation differs from empowerment, which is the ability to change your state of being, including your feelings and behavior, for the better. Adults who seek validation more than empowerment (and growth) will end up disappointed no matter what they get. Feeling validated brings only a brief sense of well-being, unless we're able (empowered) to respond compassionately in return and otherwise actively improve our own emotional states.

Emotional validation is not growth. By definition, emotional growth is transcending the limitations of our painful experience. In other words, emotional validation is not an end but, at best, a precursor to healing and growth. An enriched life comes from the ability to self-regulate, which enables us to see many perspectives, in addition to our own experience.

Even When Seemingly Supported by Research, It's Wrong

Though far more sophisticated than the pop-psychology notion of emotional needs, an influential movement in couples counseling similarly promotes Toddler-brain relationships. This unfortunate byproduct of well-meaning counseling draws support from the theoretical work of the British psychiatrist John Bowlby, known as "attachment theory."

The essence of Bowlby's work is empirically supported by observations of toddlers. A follower of his, researcher Mary Ainsworth, devised a study of how toddlers cope with a 20-minute period of separation from their mothers, during which they were visited by a nonthreatening stranger, who subsequently left after the mothers returned. Ainsworth conceived distinct "attachment styles," based on how the children reacted to their mothers when they came back. According to her classifications, children who were *securely attached* to their mothers played freely while their mothers were present, using them as a "safe base" from which to explore the environment. They were visibly upset when the mothers departed but happy to see them upon their return. Ainsworth concluded that the children felt confident that their mothers were available and would be responsive to their attachment needs.

Children with the *anxious-avoidant insecure attachment* style avoided or ignored their mothers—showing little emotion when they departed or returned. These children did not explore very much with their mothers present or absent.

Toddlers classified as *anxious-ambivalent/resistant* showed distress even before separation, and were clingy and difficult to comfort on the mother's return. They either showed signs of resentment in response to her absence or signs of helpless passivity.

Ainsworth refined and subdivided the categories over the years, but the core distinction between secure and insecure attachment styles remained intact. It should be noted that there is some controversy concerning Ainsworth's methods. Some researchers have pointed out that she confounds temperament with attachment style. These are difficult to distinguish at any age, but especially in toddlers.

Though attachment theory has utility in understanding parent-child relational development, its application to adult love relationships is more problematic. Describing it as a "science of love," as some authors do, is downright misleading. The empirical support for that description is the Adult Attachment Interview (AAI), developed by researcher Mary Main.

The AAI was designed to predict the quality of parental responsiveness to their infant's attachment needs, based on their recollection of their attachment to their own caregivers. When their recollections are coded to fit Ainsworth's attachment styles, there is, indeed, a correlation between the parents' recollections and their current parenting style.

Two problems emerge in using the AAI as a research foundation for adult love relationships. The obvious one is that its predicative validity is stronger for parenting than for adult intimate relationships. The second problem is more serious. The AAI (and its derivations) use the recollections of adult interviewees to construct a model of their early childhood experience. Distant recollections are highly influenced by how people feel at the moment they make the recollections. Independent research shows that what people recall is more about the way they make sense of their lives now than what they actually experienced as very young children.

Other research on adult attachment styles feature question-naires that at least focus on how people behave in their current relationships. However, using these classifications as a foundation for relationship therapy tends to obscure the power of interactive dynamics that have become habitually laced with blame, denial, and avoidance. The habituation of blame, denial, and avoidance as coping mechanisms is *independent* of attachment styles.

Applying research findings about parent-child interactions to the complexities of adult intimate relationships should raise a few red flags. Therapeutic approaches that do so ineluctably foster Toddler-brain love. Yet many practitioners encourage partners to take turns meeting each other's toddler needs of mirroring and validation, in the hopes of manufacturing a secure attachment style that was apparently absent in actual toddlerhood.

Even if self-regulation deficits in adults were caused by early parent-child interactions—and we have no way of knowing that for certain—asking adults to use techniques appropriate for young children with an underdeveloped sense of self strains credibility. Most adults in distressed relationships have a sense of self that doesn't require continual mirroring or validation from other people. Encouraging them to seek it creates a false perception of emotional need that will cause them nothing but misery in their relationships.

Even if it were possible that adult therapy could fill in gaps in emotional development, any kind of stress will activate the old Toddler-brain habits. By the time we're adults, emotion regulation methods are clearly habituated. Regardless of what started them, habits become entrenched through repetition, which strengthens the neural connections that underlie them. Once habits are entrenched, it doesn't matter what started them; only new habits can replace them.

Unless you're comfortable regarding your partner alternatively as a parent and a toddler, using the parent-child model for adult relationships makes little sense. It ignores the fact that the prefrontal cortex develops many years after toddlerhood to regulate the way we cope with stress. As it matures, it is able to replace blame, deny, and avoid with improve, appreciate, connect, protect, and nurture, all of which are Adult-brain activities central to adult love. The whole point of parent-child attachment is to raise children to be self-regulating adults, able to nurture their own children, not to remain forever childish by continually reinforcing Toddler-brain feelings, impulses, and perceived emotional needs to be mirrored and validated.

Please understand, I'm not saying that feelings driven by the Toddler brain aren't important—quite the opposite. *All* your feelings are important, not just the ones you experience at any given moment, which the Toddler brain wants mirrored and validated. The stability of your feelings, indeed your entire well-being, depends heavily on fidelity to your deeper values, not on validating and mirroring the feeling of the moment. The latter, at best, makes you lose sight of the forest for the trees. At worst, it turns you into a different person whenever your feelings change.

I doubt that very many adults really want to be treated like a child or want a lover who must be treated like one. The way we love in the Adult brain differs radically from the way we love in the Toddler brain. Thank God.

In the Toddler brain, I only want you to mirror my experience of the world and I react negatively when you have your own thoughts, feelings, and behaviors that do not match my experience. *Power love* is sustained by compassion, kindness, appreciation of differences, and adherence to deeper values.

INDEX

abandonment, fear of, 67
abusive relationships, 40, 134
adrenaline, 151
    arousal, 87, 88
    contempt and, 115, 127
    emotions and, 47, 145
Adult Attachment Interview (AAI), 220
Adult brain, compassion in, 109
    core vulnerabilities and, 4, 18,
        106, 115, 128, 133–138, 203–204
    creating value in, 173
    disagreements and, 138, 211
    intimate relationships in, 71–80
    negotiating specific behaviors, 132
    obsession and, 107
    value conflicts in, 86
Adult-brain resolution, 86
aggression, 26
Ainsworth, Mary, 219–220
anger, 106
animals, emotional reactivity in, 14
    pack behavior, 14, 63
    social bonds, 6
anxiety, and touch, 161
anxiety regulation, 129–130
appreciation, 140
"Approach" motivation, 161
arousal, emotional, 122
    negative, 122
attachment, emotional, 36
attachment emotions, function of, 106
attachment styles, 219
attachment theory, 219, 220
attitude of connection, in Adult brain, 192
    in Toddler brain, 190
attunement, emotional, 161
automatic defense system, 15, 57
    hypersensitivity in, 16
autonomy, 6, 11
autonomy and connection, 140, 210
autonomy-connection struggle, 87, 96
avoidance, 23, 24, 39

behavior, automatic, 61
    divorce-predictive, 39

egalitarian, xi
    fear-avoidant, 61
    habitual, xii
    passive-aggressive, 33, 34, 56
    reward-seeking, 49
behaviors, self-defeating, 31
    value-enhancing, 151
binocular vision, 117–125, 211
blame, 23, 24, 25, 32, 79, 103, 143, 145
blame, and adrenaline, 25
    social function of, 25
blind spots, 77, 78, 122
body language, 15, 57, 161
bonding hormones, 177
Bowen, Murray, 11
Bowlby, John, 219
brain, adult, viii
    adult activities of, 27
    cognitive limits in toddler, 3
    interplay between adult and toddler,
        147
    late maturity in adult, 8
    mammalian, and repetition, 147
    primary features of adult, 7
    toddler, vii
    upper prefrontal cortex, xii
Burton, Robert A., 47

chaos, fear of, 67–68
"climate" of a relationship, 101–102
closeness and distance, 101
coercion, 63, 162
cognitive dissonance, 20
common values, 193
communication, 18
    and disconnection, 160
    high emotional reactivity and, 18
    techniques, 159
    verbal, 19
compassion, 72, 75, 109
    ending relationships, 114
    fear of, 73
compassionate assertiveness, 74
conditioned responses, vii, 182
conflict, emotional, 4